Wild cat *Felis silvestris*

Lynx *Lynx lynx*

Common genet
Genetta genetta

Domestic cat *Felis domesticus*

Western polecat
Mustela putorius

Mink *Mustela vison*

Wolverine *Gulo gulo*

Stoat *Mustela erminea*

Weasel *Mustela nivalis*

Badger *Meles meles*

Otter *Lutra lutra*

Fox
Vulpes vulpes

Wolf
Canis lupus

Raccoon *Procyon lotor*

Raccoon dog
Nyctereutes procyonoides

Brown bear *Ursus arctos*

Common seal *Phoca vitulina*

Animal Tracks and Signs

Animal Tracks and Signs

TEXT BY
PREBEN BANG

ILLUSTRATIONS BY
PREBEN DAHLSTRØM

FOREWORD BY
RAY MEARS

Translated by Network Communications
and edited by Martin Walters

OXFORD
UNIVERSITY PRESS

Great Clarendon Street, Oxford OX2 6DP
Oxford University Press is a department of the University of Oxford.
It furthers the University's objective of excellence in research, scholarship,
and education by publishing worldwide in
Oxford
New York
Auckland Bangkok Buenos Aires Cape Town Chennai Dar es Salaam Delhi
Hong Kong Istanbul Karachi Kolkata Kuala Lumpur Madrid Melbourne
Mexico City Mumbai Nairobi São Paulo Shanghai Taipei Tokoy Toronto

Oxford is a registered trade mark of Oxford University Press
in the UK and in certain other countries

Published in the United States
by Oxford University Press, Inc., New York

English edition © Oxford University Press 2001

Translated from *Dyrespor: Fra pattedyr og fugle*
© Gyldendalske Boghandel, Nordisk Forlag A/S, Denmark 1997

The moral rights of the author have been asserted

Database right Oxford University Press (maker)

First published 2001
Reprinted 2003, 2004
Reissued 2006

British Library Cataloguing in Publication Data
Data available

Library of Congress Cataloging in Publication Data availble

ISBN 0-19-929997-8
ISBN 978-0-19-929997-3

Typeset by Narayana Press
Printed by South Sea International Press. Hong Kong
Paper: 130 g Nopa Coat mat.

Table of contents

Lynx track in the mountains.

Foreword by Ray Mears

Life has little to offer that is more challenging and rewarding than finding the trail of a wild animal and following it to the animal itself. But this ancient skill is not quickly learned, it requires practice, determination and above all else time outdoors.

Tracking is more a way of thinking than a skill. A tracker needs to establish a mental link with the thing they are following. This intuitive understanding of how the quarry behaves and how it moves enables the tracker to anticipate the location of the next track and predict the quarry's intentions. Of course there are great distances on the trail where no tracks can be discerned, but instead only delicate traces, a few grains of sand temporarily embedded in the underside of a leaf, a fallen petal picked up from where it fell and deposited in a new location or perhaps soft rush stems brushed in the direction of the animal's travel and held enmeshed, pointing the way until a strong breeze untangles them. These and countless other signs are the real meat of tracking, but to spot these signs the tracker must first be able to recognise and correctly interpret the more easily read traces such as footprints, droppings, and feeding signs.

In the following pages you will discover a remarkable field guide to these signs and traces. In sharing their knowledge and enthusiasm for animal tracks and signs the author Preben Bang and illustrator Preben Dahlstrøm unwittingly compiled a seminal work, setting an example of format and layout for this type of field guide that has been wisely emulated by tracking specialists in the preparation of field guides for other parts of the world. There is no better place to learn to track than in your own backyard: my advice is to keep this guide handy when you are outdoors and seek out all of the signs and tracks it contains. By the time the book is committed to memory and the memories are set by experience you will have learned far more than just tracking.

On a personal note this book more than any other set me on my own exploration of tracking. A journey which has led me to explore many different wildernesses and to learn from indigenous trackers around the globe. Now when I travel in wild places spotting the tracks of bears, lions, jaguars or wolves does more than just help me travel safely; it enables me to connect with the landscape around me, reading the hidden mysteries of these creatures' nocturnal lives in fascination rather than fear. But you should be warned, there is no end to the study of animal tracking and the pursuit of sign is addictive!

Preface

People view nature in many different ways. Some enjoy the 'big picture' – the shapes, the colours, the sounds and the wide-open spaces. Others gain particular pleasure from spotting and identifying a certain bird or plant. Yet others have great fun investigating nature's 'clues' in the same way that a detective searches the scene of a crime for 'clues' to the perpetrator. The clues referred to in this book are all the pieces of evidence (be they large or small) showing that some kind of animal has been there before you, e.g. a footprint, a tree with the bark torn off, a broken snail shell etc. In many cases these signs are all you will actually see of wild animals – especially mammals, which are either nocturnal or very shy.

Animal Tracks is primarily aimed at the latter group of countryside visitors, but it is hoped that others will also find it interesting.

You could make finding tracks your primary goal when visiting the countryside, and do research in advance on the type of tracks you expect to find. On the other hand, you could take a more casual approach – you are almost bound to run across an unmistakable sign sooner or later, provided you are aware that they exist. In either case, a book like *Animal Tracks* comes in very handy.

We hope that *Animal Tracks* will provide a starting point for enjoyable wildlife experiences, and will help further your knowledge about the lives of animals.

The editor

Introduction

For people who survive by hunting, recognising animal tracks and signs is a matter of life or death. The hunter must be totally familiar with the signs animals leave behind, so that he is in no doubt about which tracks are worth following and where he should set his traps. Hunters require intimate knowledge of the animals' way of life and habits, for without this they simply would not be able to survive.

In modern society, knowledge of animals' behaviour is much less important.

However, for foresters, farmers and gardeners it is extremely important to be able to determine (based on the different tracks the animals leave) what species of animal has damaged their trees or eaten their crops. They will then be able to protect their financial interests without causing suffering to innocent animals.

Nowadays more and more people head out into the countryside in their leisure time in search of rest and recreation. This has led to great interest in plants and animals, and increasing awareness of the fact that protecting wildlife is necessary for our existence.

Although it is easy to observe and enjoy plants, which stay put once they have taken root, it is much harder to manage to see mammals, the larger ones in particular. Firstly, most of them are nocturnal or twilight animals, and, secondly, they are very shy and will vanish at the slightest noise. However, their presence is revealed in many ways, through footprints, droppings, feeding signs etc. If you take a look at these and try interpreting them, you will discover that they can tell you a great deal about the animal's life and behaviour.

Most tracks and signs remain for only a short time, generally disappearing very rapidly. However, as the picture on this page shows, under particularly favourable conditions they can be preserved for years, sometimes many thousands of years. In Southern France, for instance, a 15-20,000-year old fossilised footprint of the long-extinct cave bear has been found. In bogs in Denmark 'beaver sticks', branches with distinct beaver teeth marks, have been found (see page 121); the beaver vanished from Denmark in prehistoric times. In the bogs you can also find bones and antlers that bear clear signs of having been gnawed several thousand years ago.

An elk antler, more than 5,000 years old, showing clear marks of having been gnawed by a squirrel.

How to use this book

To make this a useful field guide, the individual prints have been arranged according to type, and then according to animal, i.e. the main sections of the book follow the types of signs: footprints, feeding signs etc., and the sub-sections (apart from a few exceptions) are arranged according to animal groups. The animals are generally listed in systematic order – starting with the most 'primitive' and ending with the most 'advanced'.

1. When you find *footprints, partly-eaten cones or other fruit, droppings* or *pellets*:

First, decide which of the aforementioned types it is. Then, look up the relevant type, and you will find a plate showing numerous examples to help you further. For instance, if you find a partly-eaten hazelnut, look up 'feeding signs' and you will find a plate that includes illustrations of various feeding marks on hazelnuts. By comparing the actual nut with the illustrations you can determine on the spot which animal was responsible. The plate gives page references for further details. By reading the details and comparing your find with the illustrations you can check whether your first identification was correct.

With pad tracks you should note that all the pads are shown on the track plates, but you will not usually be able to see all of them in the actual footprint. The grey area indicates the size of the entire foot.

2. For *signs of gnawing on trees and bushes, remains from a kill, homes and hiding places* and *other signs* that are impractical to illustrate on plates, you will find the relevant topic in the table of contents.

3. If you want to know which tracks and signs *are included* for a particular animal, look in the index.

4. An explanation of the *system used for the print drawings* is given on page 28.

FOOT PRINTS

Animals' footprints can be observed best when the ground is covered in snow. The ideal snow is fine-grained, not too wet, melting snow on a hard, level foundation such as a road or an expanse of ice or hard snow a few centimetres thick. This will provide very distinct and well-defined footprints, and the characteristic details of the different tracks will be clearly marked and easy to read. In loose, freezing snow the outlines of the prints will generally collapse, obliterating the prints themselves, and if the layer of snow is too thick, the prints will be deep holes that are difficult to interpret.

When analysing tracks it is important to realise that a print in loose, freezing snow will almost always be significantly larger than one left on a more solid foundation. You should also be aware that tracks become enlarged very rapidly during a thaw, especially if the sun is shining, as the edges will melt away quickest. In these instances you can easily be led to believe that the track comes from a much larger animal than it actually does.

When there is no snow it is much more difficult to find and identify animal tracks. It takes a trained eye to detect that an animal has run across a forest floor carpeted with dead leaves or crossed a grass-covered field or meadow, and in most cases this is only possible if it was a large, heavy animal.

Therefore for most of the year you have to look for animal tracks in spots with no vegetation, and preferably after rainy spells,

when the ground is damp. The best prints can generally be found in moist, slightly loamy soil. However, you can also find excellent tracks in wet sand along shorelines at low tide, and you can often find clear tracks in dunes too, early in the morning while the sand is still wet with dew. Later in the day, as the sand dries out, it will collapse and obliterate the tracks. Forest tracks and recently dried-out ditches in woods are also good places to look for footprints, and in dried-up puddles with a thin, fine layer of mud over a solid foundation you will often find some of the most distinct tracks, particularly those of smaller animals.

The best way to get to know a track is to make a sketch of it, including accurate dimensions (see page 41). This forces you to take note of all the details of the track, and you therefore remember them better. A quicker but less effective method is to photograph it. To be able to judge the size in the photograph it is very important to include a scale object in the picture – something that is often omitted. If you feel this spoils the picture, take two, one with and one without the scale object.

Footprint plates

The drawings on the following pages can be used for initial identification of a footprint. Use the page references for further information. Please note that not all the footprints mentioned are shown on the plates.

Actual size

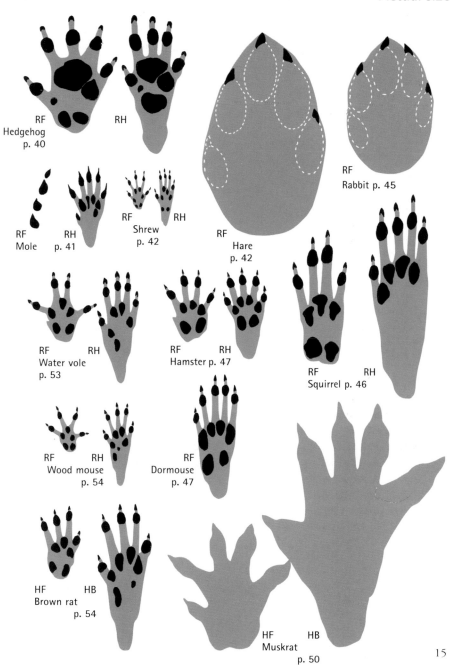

RF
Hedgehog
p. 40

RH

RF
Mole

RH
p. 41

RF
Shrew
p. 42

RH

RF
Hare
p. 42

RF
Rabbit p. 45

RF
Water vole
p. 53

RH

RF
Hamster p. 47

RH

RF
Squirrel p. 46

RH

RF
Wood mouse
p. 54

RH

RF
Dormouse
p. 47

HF
Brown rat
p. 54

HB

HF
Muskrat
p. 50

HB

15

Approx. ²/₃ actual size

RH   RF
Beaver
p. 49

RF
Coypu

RH
p. 50

Actual size

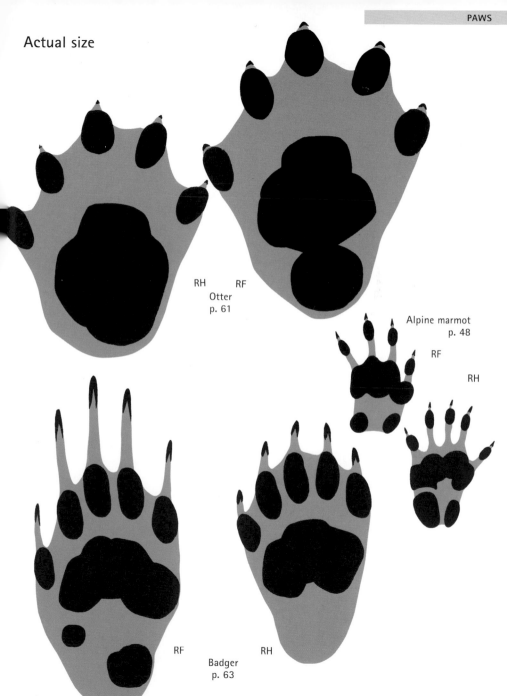

RH   RF

Otter
p. 61

Alpine marmot
p. 48

RF

RH

RF

Badger
p. 63

RH

Actual size

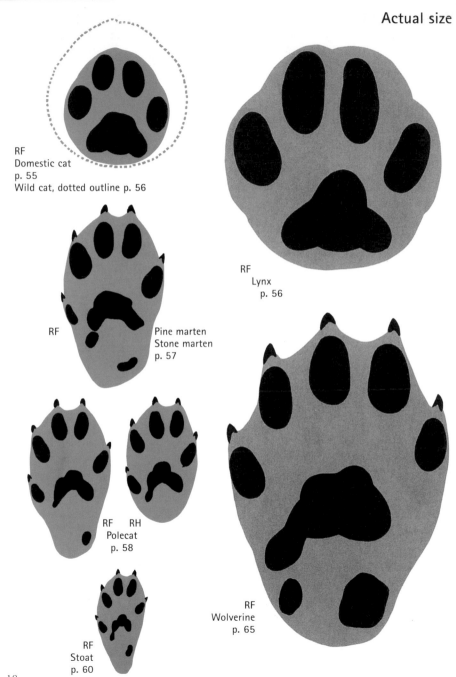

RF
Domestic cat
p. 55
Wild cat, dotted outline p. 56

RF
Lynx
p. 56

RF

Pine marten
Stone marten
p. 57

RF   RH
Polecat
p. 58

RF
Wolverine
p. 65

RF
Stoat
p. 60

Varying scales

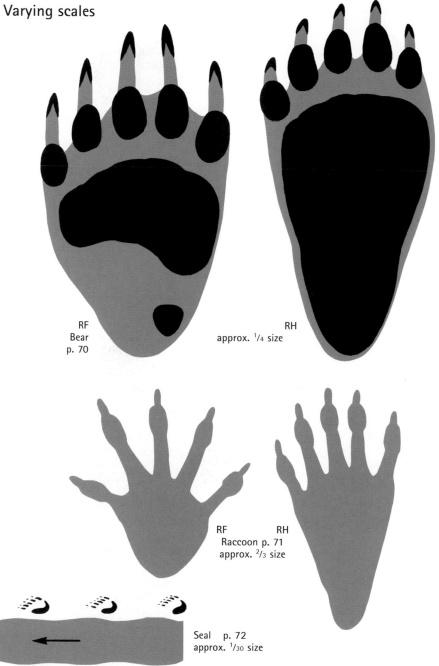

RF
Bear
p. 70

RH

approx. ¼ size

RF   RH

Raccoon p. 71
approx. ²/₃ size

Seal   p. 72
approx. ¹/₃₀ size

19

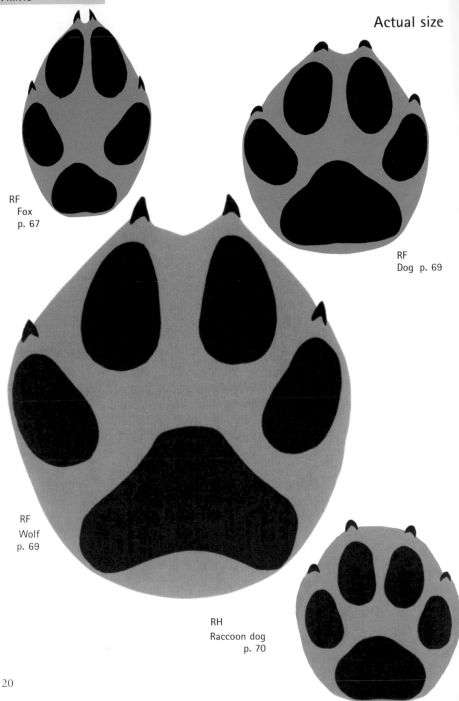

Actual size

RF
Fox
p. 67

RF
Dog p. 69

RF
Wolf
p. 69

RH
Raccoon dog
p. 70

Actual size

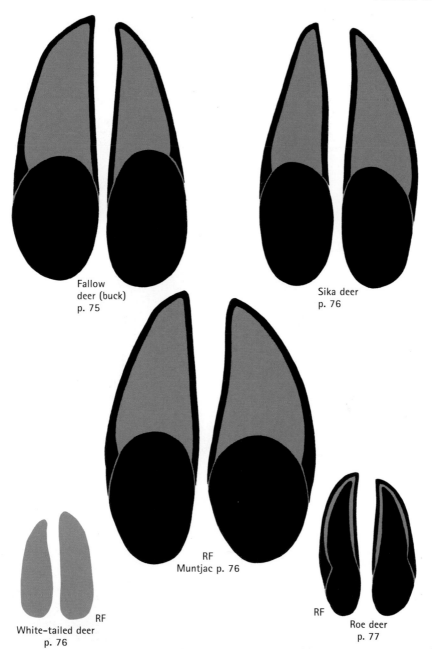

Fallow
deer (buck)
p. 75

Sika deer
p. 76

RF
Muntjac p. 76

RF
White-tailed deer
p. 76

RF
Roe deer
p. 77

21

Actual size

RF
Wild boar p. 73

RF
Red deer
(hind)
p. 74

RF
Red deer
(stag)
p. 74

Varying scales

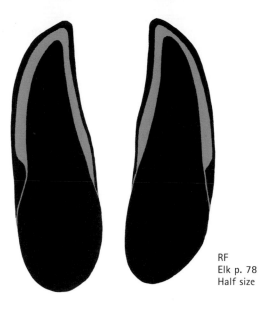

RF
Elk p. 78
Half size

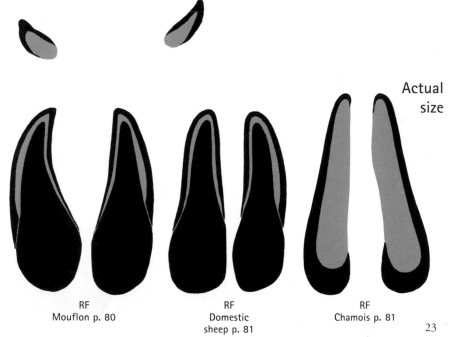

Actual size

RF
Mouflon p. 80

RF
Domestic
sheep p. 81

RF
Chamois p. 81

23

Varying scales

RF
Reindeer p. 80
Half size

RF
Domestic goat p. 82
Actual size

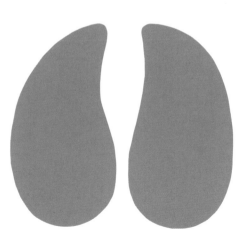

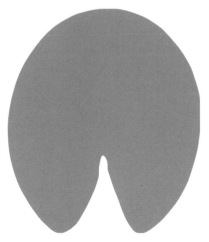

Domestic cow p. 83
approx. ²/₃ size

Horse p. 84
approx. ¹/₂ size

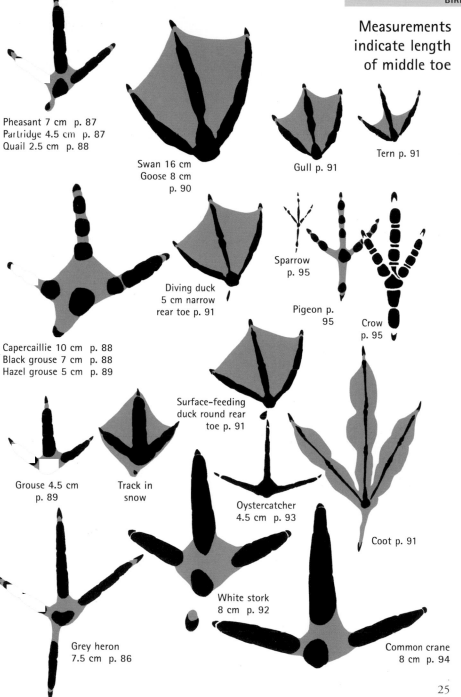

Measurements
indicate length
of middle toe

Pheasant 7 cm p. 87
Partridge 4.5 cm p. 87
Quail 2.5 cm p. 88

Swan 16 cm
Goose 8 cm
p. 90

Gull p. 91

Tern p. 91

Sparrow
p. 95

Diving duck
5 cm narrow
rear toe p. 91

Pigeon p.
95

Crow
p. 95

Capercaillie 10 cm p. 88
Black grouse 7 cm p. 88
Hazel grouse 5 cm p. 89

Surface-feeding
duck round rear
toe p. 91

Grouse 4.5 cm
p. 89

Track in
snow

Oystercatcher
4.5 cm p. 93

Coot p. 91

White stork
8 cm p. 92

Grey heron
7.5 cm p. 86

Common crane
8 cm p. 94

25

Tracks of a fox – first walking with uneven steps (right), then jumping (left)

Mammal footprints

Foot structure

A mammal's footprint reproduces the structure and shape of the sole of the foot in what is known as hollow relief. To be able to identify a track, it is therefore necessary to know a little about the structure and appearance of the feet of the different animal species.

The feet of plantigrade animals

Early mammals had five clawed toes on all four feet and were plantigrade, i.e. they walked on the entire sole of the foot. This primitive foot type can be found almost unchanged in most of the insectivores; the hedgehog and the shrew being typical examples. It can also be found in other mammals, e.g. badgers and bears.

In animals with five well-developed toes, these are always of different lengths. The toes are numbered from 1 to 5, beginning with the inside toe (equivalent to the thumb on a human hand) and ending with the outside toe (the little finger). No. 3 is the longest, then comes no. 4, no. 2, the outside toe (no. 5), and finally the inside toe (no. 1). Thus the inside toe is the shortest, which means that if you have a print with an imprint of all five toes and the shortest toe is on the left-hand side, the print was made by the right foot. In many instances the inside toe leaves only a faint impression – sometimes none at all – and the print has four unequally long toes, the shortest then being the outside toe.

Plantigrades are relatively short-legged animals that normally move at a leisurely pace, as their foot structure is not well suited to bounding or running over long distances. For an animal to be able to run fast and far, it must have long legs, and the foot's area of contact with the ground must be as small as possible. We know this from our own experi-

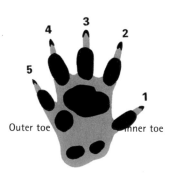

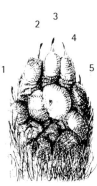

Hedgehog. Left, imprint of right forepaw with toes numbered. Right, underside of the same paw.

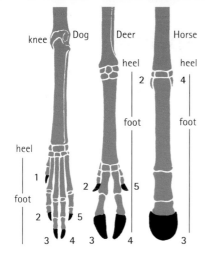

Foot structure of dog, deer and horse. A pig's foot corresponds to that of a deer. Note the different position of the midfoot in relation to the ground. The numbers indicate the toes.

ence: when walking, the entire sole of our foot touches the ground, but when running, we only use the front part of our foot, the toes and the ball of the foot.

The feet of digitigrade animals

Over time a number of foot types have evolved from the plantigrade foot, adapted for different types of movement and speeds – running, jumping etc. Those that often travel at a run are digitigrade (e.g. cats) or unguligrade (e.g. deer). They step with only their toes or the tips of their toes touching the ground, and through the development of the leg bones – whereby certain of the foot bones have been greatly extended – these animals have gained long, slender limbs. There has also been a reduction in the number of toes, and those remaining – or some of them – have usually changed

substantially. The most frequent occurrence is a reduction of toe no. 1 (the thumb), which often completely disappears so the animal becomes four-toed. A reduction of toes no. 2 and no. 5 is also fairly common (unguligrade), as in deer, for example, where these toes have turned into small dew claws (also called side toes or dew claws). In horses, all the toes except no. 3 have disappeared, and the animal steps only on the outermost hoof-covered part.

Pads

Pads are there to protect the underside of the foot; these are thick, elastic connective tissue pads covered with a strong but soft horny layer. They have sweat glands, and the secretion from these may be left in the tracks, giving them a scent. The pads are hairless, but in most animals the skin in between is covered in hair, and in some cases, for example the pine marten and the squirrel, the covering of hair can be so thick in the winter that it completely covers the pads. The hare does not have pads; they have been replaced by a dense, resilient layer of strong, stiff

Underside of a hare's paw, showing the dense layer of hair.

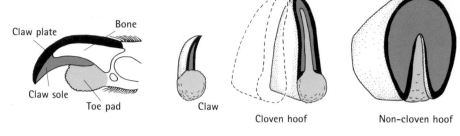

Claw plate
Bone
Claw sole
Toe pad
Claw
Cloven hoof
Non-cloven hoof

Toes and tips of digits are protected by a horny layer, which is also useful for various other practical purposes, e.g. for gripping, for digging, for killing prey etc. The claw is an early adaptation, while the cloven and non-cloven hoof are later developments.

hairs. Obviously a strong growth of hair on the sole of an animal's foot will blot out many of the details of the track.

There is one *toe (digital) pad* under the tip of each toe, and along the front edge of the midfoot a transverse row of *middle (interdigital) pads* – one for each toe space. In many animals the middle pads have more or less merged. Dogs, foxes, badgers and cats have one large pad, which is often referred to as the central pad. In some animals you will also find, on the midfoot section of the fore foot behind the intermediate pads, one – sometimes two – *carpal (proximal) pads.*

Types of prints

Animal footprints can be divided into three groups according to foot structure: paw prints, cloven hoof prints and non-cloven hoof prints. Below are brief descriptions of these three groups. The different prints within each group are dealt with in more detail from page 40 onwards.

Paw prints

Important details to note in tracks made by paws are the number of paws, the shape and size of the claws and pads and their position relative to one another.

Whether you can see any imprint from the claws will depend not only on the quality of the soil but also to a great extent on the size of the claws and their position on the toes. The large, long, digging claws of a badger's fore foot always stand out clearly in tracks, but you will never see claw marks in a cat or lynx track, as a tensile ligament keeps them raised and concealed, so they do not touch the ground while the animal is moving and only appear when the toes are curled.

The fore and hind foot may have differing structures, and will therefore leave different tracks. Here is a typical rodent example.

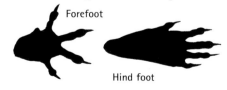

Forefoot

Hind foot

The print from the fore foot is broader, deeper and more clearly outlined than that from the hind foot in almost all animals other than rodents. In addition, during slow movement the toes on the fore foot will be more splayed than those on the hind foot. This is easy to ascertain by measuring the distance between the claws of the middle toes. If the animal is moving quickly, this will be more marked.

Each individual footprint shows in which direction the animal was moving, and in most cases this is not difficult to determine. In deep snow, where prints are fairly deep, the back edges will taper down while the front edges will be more vertical, usually with snow thrown up at the front by the foot.

Measuring: The length of a paw is always measured from the front edge of the pad on the longest toe to the rear edge of the central middle pad. The claws are not included. If the entire print is visible, an additional measurement can be taken, out to the very back edge. The width is measured at the track's widest point. To obtain measurements of the greatest possible accuracy, use a print made by an animal moving slowly. At faster speeds the feet tend to skid slightly, which can easily make the measurements too large.

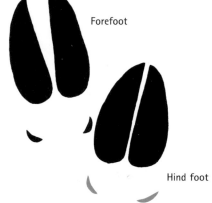

Toes of a cloven-hoofed animal, here a deer, with corresponding imprints. As mentioned in the text, the side toes (side hoofs) do not always leave an imprint.

Side toes

Middle toes

2   5

3   4

Forefoot

Hind foot

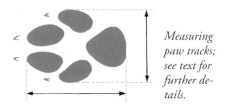

Measuring paw tracks; see text for further details.

Cloven-hoof prints

Cloven-hoofed animals have a very distinctive foot that leaves easily recognisable tracks. They have four toes (toe no. 1 is missing) but step only on the tips of no. 3 and no. 4, i.e. the middle toes (cleaves), which are greatly developed and almost totally symmetrical. Toes 2 and 5, the dew claws, are much smaller and have shifted to the back of the foot. In most instances they are so far up the leg they do not touch the ground during ordinary walking. Only when the animal treads on soft earth or snow, or when

31

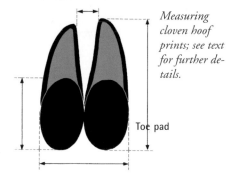

Measuring cloven hoof prints; see text for further details.

Toe pad

the ankle joints give way when running or jumping, do marks from the dew claws appear in the track. However, the wild boar and the reindeer are exceptions to this, as their dew claws are so low that they also touch the ground during normal walking.

Each cleave of a cloven hoof is made up of a *plate* and a *sole*. The plate forms the cleave's smooth, curved topside, and the sole the underside on which the animal treads. The plate generally projects out over the sole and forms a sharp edge (wall) that is clearly visible in the track. On very hard ground the imprint from this edge is often all you will see. Behind the sole is the toe pad, which forms a greater or lesser part of the underside of each cleave. In very distinct tracks, from red deer, fallow deer or reindeer, for example, the toe pad will stand out as a rounded depression. In roe deer and elk the sole has almost disappeared and the toe pad extends to the tip of the cleave.

When identifying a track from a cloven-footed animal the first thing to note is the shape and size of the cleave. With very clear imprints the size of the toe pad may also be significant. The imprints from the two large cleaves have almost straight inner edges

while the outer edges are somewhat curved, and the imprints are practically mirror images of one another. However, sometimes the two digits on the same foot are not of equal size; in these instances the inner digit is almost always the shortest.

The print from the fore foot is larger and heavier than that from the hind foot, and, in addition, the digits on the fore foot will splay slightly during steady movement, while the digits on the hind feet may merge almost completely. During rapid movement this will be even more marked, as the front cleaves will spread in a V-shape. This is also true of the dew claws, which always leave the clearest and largest imprint in the fore print. **Measuring:** When measuring a cloven hoof print, find one made by an animal moving at a steady pace and measure the length, width and distance between the cleave tips, and – if possible – the length of the toe pad.

Non-cloven hoof prints

There are no wild animals with non-cloven hooves in Europe. However, this type of track is mentioned briefly, as you will frequently come across tracks from horses, mules and

Structure and imprint of horse's foot.

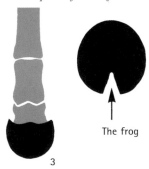

The frog

3

donkeys. The horse has just one toe, no. 3, on each leg, and steps only on the outer toe joint, which has an extremely well-developed hoof. Like the cloven hoof, it is actually a modified claw. It curves round the little toe pad, and the track left is almost circular.

Gaits

When identifying a track, in addition to noting the characteristics of the individual prints, it is often very useful to look at their pattern, i.e. the way the individual prints are positioned in relation to one another (assuming that you have a string of prints, which is often not the case in the summer, although it always occurs when the ground is covered in snow). The tracks of many animals form such distinctive patterns that it is possible to make out what the animal is from a distance and without closer examination of the footprints. In cases where the individual footprints are indistinct and no details are visible, the pattern of the tracks can therefore be decisive in identification.

This pattern reflects the animal's way of moving and shows what gait was used. So once you can recognise the patterns that correspond to the different gaits, you will be able to read whether the animal was walking, trotting or launched into a jump or gallop. Once you have mastered this, it becomes more interesting to follow an animal track, as you can gain a more vivid impression of what the animal was doing. For

Galloping horses. Horses 2 and 3 are not in contact with the ground at all.

instance, you can see where it walked steadily forward, where it crept cautiously towards its prey and where it took off at full speed.

If you want to get to know the various gaits, it is useful to observe domesticated animals and look at the tracks they leave when they move in different ways. It is easy to see how they place their feet in relation to one another when moving slowly, but if they are moving fast it is impossible to follow the movements in detail. In film of equestrian events and horse races on TV however, you often have the opportunity to watch the animals cross the finishing line in slow motion. This offers excellent opportunities for observing how they move their legs when travelling at a fast pace.

There are four main types of gait: walking (step), trotting, galloping and jumping/bounding.

Walking

The characteristic feature of walking is that the four feet are lifted and placed on the ground at different times, none of the legs moving together. So when a horse walks on a hard road, you hear the individual hoofbeats clearly distinct from one another. It moves its legs in a fairly specific sequence, and looks as if it is constantly trying to tread on its own heels. If it starts with its right hind leg, for instance, the others follow in this order: right foreleg, left hind leg, left foreleg; and then the right hind leg again, and so on.

The hind foot is always set down close to the print of the fore foot so that the print from the hind foot is either just in front, just behind or on top of the fore print. In this last instance, where the fore print is more or less covered, the pattern of the track is known as 'foot in foot'. This method is used regularly by deer, but many other ani-

Tracks and stride lengths for different gaits.

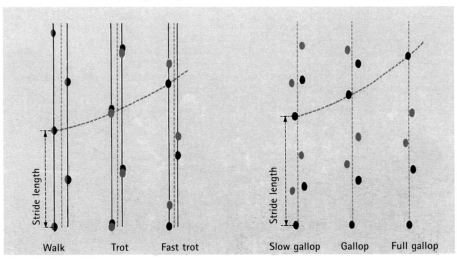

Stride length

Walk   Trot   Fast trot

Stride length

Slow gallop   Gallop   Full gallop

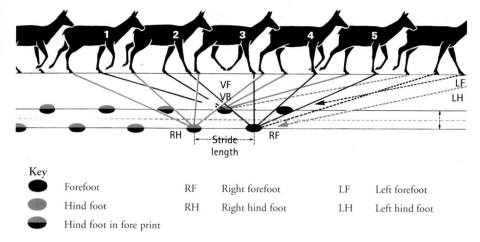

Key

⬤	Forefoot	RF	Right forefoot	LF	Left forefoot
⬤	Hind foot	RH	Right hind foot	LH	Left hind foot
⬤	Hind foot in fore print				

Typical movement pattern when walking (deer).

1. The animal begins a stride with its right hind foot in the right fore print. The right forefoot has just left the ground. The left forefoot is on the ground, and the animal rests diagonally on the right hind leg and left foreleg.
2. The right forefoot is placed on the ground, and the animal is now supported by three legs: right hind leg, right foreleg and left foreleg.
3. The left hind foot is brought forward and, before it is placed on the ground in the left fore print, the left forefoot is lifted. The animal now rests on two legs on the same side.

4. The left hind foot is placed on the ground. The left forefoot is brought forward, and the animal is again supported by three legs: left hind leg, right hind leg and right foreleg.
5. The right hind foot is lifted, and the animal now rests again on two legs: left hind leg and right foreleg. The position is as in 1, but the opposite diagonal. The next foot to be placed on the ground will be the left forefoot, followed by the right hind foot, and so on.

mals also use it – particularly in deep snow, where it is obviously easiest for the animal to place its hind foot in the hole already made by the fore foot.

When an animal moves at a walk, the footprints produce two distinctly separate parallel rows. The stride length is the distance between two successive footprints from the same foot, and the straddle is the distance between the right and left side tracks. The print pattern at a walk is characterised by a short stride and a clear straddle.

With the special gait known as ambling, the foreleg and hind leg on the same side move simultaneously. This gait, which is familiar from camels, can very occasionally be observed in horses, dogs and cats.

Trotting

Trotting is a substantially faster movement than walking. Its characteristic feature is that the foreleg on one side and the hind leg on the other side move simultaneously, i.e. the right fore foot is lifted and placed on the

35

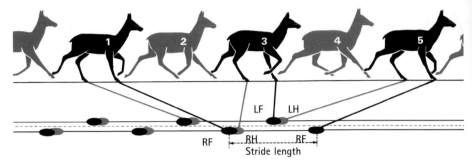

RF |←----RH----------RF----→|
Stride length

Typical trotting pattern (deer). For key see walking diagram, page 35.
1. The animal sets off diagonally with the right forefoot and left hind foot. The left hind foot is in the left fore print. The forefoot takes off just before the hind foot.
2. As the animal is poised in mid-air, the left foreleg and right hind leg are brought forward.

3. The left forefoot and right hind foot make contact with the ground simultaneously. The right hind foot is placed roughly in the right fore print, and a new take-off follows.
4. The animal rises again, and now the right foreleg and left hind leg are brought forward.
5. The right forefoot and left hind foot come into contact with the ground again. The left hind foot is placed roughly in the left fore print.

ground at the same time as the left hind foot. When a horse trots on a hard road you hear a series of beats at regular intervals, but each beat actually consists of two identical hoofbeats.

A trotting animal almost seems to glide forward. Its centre of gravity remains nearly level, with no energy expended lifting the body for each take-off. In proportion to the speed, which can be very fast, trotting is the least energy-demanding and least tiring gait.

The pattern of the tracks greatly resembles that of a walking track, but the stride length is greater and the straddle narrower, and the faster the animal trots the more marked this becomes. At a very rapid trot the right and left side tracks will be almost in line. On firm ground, the hind foot will usually strike the ground ahead of the fore print – the greater the speed the further ahead. The hind foot may also be placed in

the fore print; in snow this will almost always be the case.

Galloping

Galloping is a faster gait than bounding/jumping (see next page), and also differs in that all four legs assist in propelling the animal forward. As with jumping, during typical galloping there is a phase where the animal is airborne, but, in contrast to a jump, this follows a take-off from the forelegs. The animal lands on its hind legs, and first on one, then the other foreleg without losing contact with the ground. The four legs thus work immediately after one another.

The pattern of a typical gallop track is characterised by the fact that the individual prints are quite evenly spread and almost in line.

If speed increases during galloping, the gait becomes more like jumping. A jumping

36

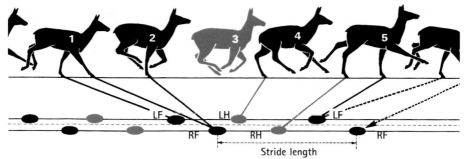

LF   LH   LF

RF   RH   RF

Stride length

Typical movement pattern for full gallop (deer). For key see walking diagram, page 35.
1. The animal rests on the left and right fore-feet, but is shifting its weight from the left fore-leg to the right. Both hind legs are moving forward.
2. The right forefoot alone bears the animal's weight for the take-off.

3. The animal is poised in mid-air for a moment, while the hind legs are brought forward.
4. The left hind foot is placed on the ground, while the right hind foot and left forefoot are brought forward.
5. The right hind foot and left forefoot now bear the animal's weight, but immediately after the right forefoot has been placed on the ground the hind legs will be in the air again, as in 1.

gallop is a cross between jumping/ bounding and galloping and is the animal's fastest gait. Here the push-off from the hind legs is also so powerful that the animal is lifted off the ground.

In a jumping gallop the animal is airborne after both the fore leg and hind leg take-off. In reality all possible transitions between jumping and galloping occur, and it is impossible to set any clear-cut boundary between these two gaits.

Jumping/bounding

Like galloping, jumping/bounding is characterised by the fact that the animal is airborne for an instant. When jumping, the animal pushes off strongly with both hind legs simultaneously, propelling it forward in an arc to land on the forelegs, which usually strike the ground one after the other. The forelegs carry the animal a little way for-

ward, prior to a weaker push-off for another bound. The hind legs then strike the ground just ahead of the fore prints, and are generally more co-ordinated. Then follows

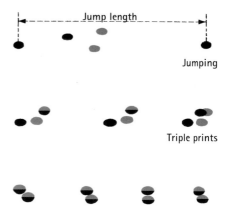

Jump length

Jumping

Triple prints

Paired prints

Tracks for various types of jump, and definition of the term jump length. See text for further details.

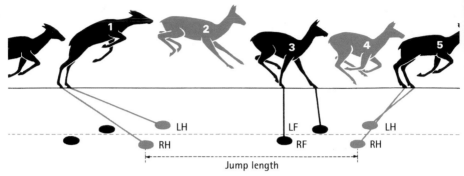

Jump length

Typical movement pattern for jumping (deer).
For key see walking diagram, page 35.
1. The animal pushes off strongly with its hind
legs.
2. The animal leaps with all four legs tucked
up beneath it. The forelegs are extended forward just before landing.

3. The right forefoot is placed on the ground
an instant before the left forefoot, which pushes
off.
4. The animal leaps with all four legs tucked
up beneath it.
5. The hind legs hit the ground and immediately push off for a new jump.

another strong push-off by the hind legs to
propel the animal forward once more. So a
jump involves a principal take-off from the
hind legs and a landing on the forelegs.

In typical jump tracks you can see the
individual footprints four and four in jump
groups. If you observe the print pattern in
the animal's direction of movement, you
will see the two fore prints just in front of
you one ahead of the other, and then the
hind prints more side by side. With marten-
type animals, where the prints in the groups
of tracks are always close to one another,
one or both of the hind feet will often overlap the fore prints, producing triple tracks
or paired tracks.

For large, heavy animals, jumping is a
very strenuous and energy-demanding form
of movement, and is therefore generally
only used in deep snow and for clearing
obstacles such as ditches, small streams,

hedges etc. On the other hand, jumping is
the most common gait for many smaller animals with long, supple backs and strong,
powerful, angled hind legs, e.g. the weasel
family and small rodents.

Measuring groups of prints

When measuring a group of tracks, it can be
useful to stretch a string down the middle –
use a few small sticks to secure it. Use the
string as a baseline, corresponding to the
grey dotted line in the preceding diagrams.

Measure the *perpendicular distance* from
the baseline to the centre of each print's
front edge and mark it on a sketch. Then
measure the *length of the group of tracks* (the
distance from the front edge of the foremost

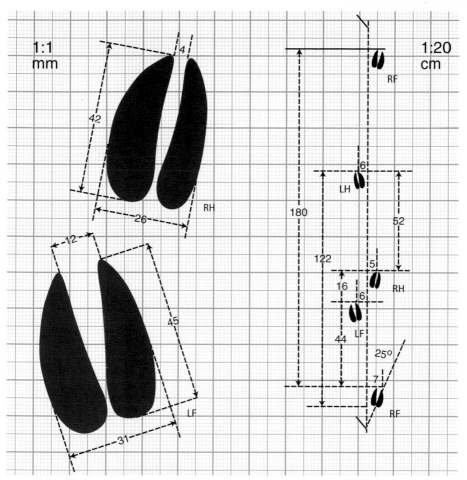

Example of how to record print and track measurements on graph paper.

print to the back edge of the hindmost print) and the *stride length* (the distance from the front edge of the foremost fore foot in a group of prints to the front edge of the corresponding print in the following group).

In addition to these measurements, you should also note on the sketch which are fore prints and which are hind prints. If some of the prints are turned outwards, indicate, as accurately as possible, the angle formed by their centre line and the baseline. It is useful to use graph paper for sketches, and, as far as possible, always use the same scale, so different sketches can be compared directly.

39

Animals with paws

For information on paw tracks and paws, see page 30.

Hedgehog
Individual prints: Hedgehogs are plantigrade, with five toes on each foot, and long claws, particularly on the hind feet. The toes and claws are clearly visible in its tracks, except the inner toe (the thumb), which even in clear tracks often leaves only a very faint mark. The tracks usually appear 4-toed. The toes on the fore feet are thick and widely splayed, the hind toes are rather more slender and closer together; the pads usually leave quite clear marks. The fore and hind prints are roughly the same size, approx. 2.5 cm long and 2.8 cm wide.
Print pattern: Hedgehogs almost always move by walking, which at faster speeds may approach a trot. The hind prints are generally behind the fore prints, but at faster speeds the hind foot may be placed more or less on top of the fore print or even slightly ahead. Stride length is short, 2-2.5 cm, but the straddle is wide, approx. 6 cm.

Hedgehog track on wet ground.

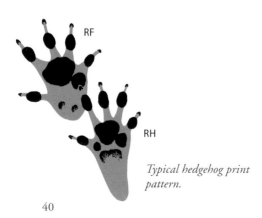

RF

RH

Typical hedgehog print pattern.

Bat
Individual prints: Bats very rarely travel on the ground, but prints can sometimes be seen in soft mud by puddles or similar where they have been down to drink.

Due to bats' special anatomy, their tracks are very distinctive, but in principle they move like other land mammals, i.e. using fore and hind limbs in diagonally opposite pairs.

The fore print always appears as a single thumb print or dot. The hind footprint displays five toes, and claw marks can usually be seen.

Bats have extremely curved thighbones, which enable them to hang head downwards. These cause the hind prints to point out at an angle from the central line of the trail.
Print pattern: When walking, the fore and hind prints appear close together, and there is a tendency for the tail to be pressed into the ground. When running, there is a sizeable gap between the fore and hind prints, and, if movement is hampered, the wingtip prints will be far apart. The tail is kept off the ground when running.

A seldom-used gait is 'frog-hopping'; the bat moves both forelimbs forward as a pair and then places the hind feet close behind. The prints lie close to the central line of the trail and at an equal distance from it. A faint tail track will also be found.

Mole

As moles live chiefly underground, their tracks are very seldom seen (see molehills, page 230).
Individual prints: Their forelegs, which are considerably modified, cannot be used in the normal walking position. The feet are twisted so the inner edge is turned downwards and the sole, which lacks pads, is turned backwards. So it treads on the front edge of the foot and on the five long, broad claws, which are visible in the track as a faint curved row of 5-6 indentations.

Various bat tracks.

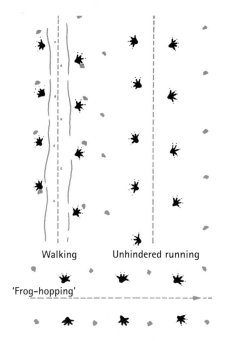

Walking   Unhindered running

'Frog-hopping'

Mole track – normal walking

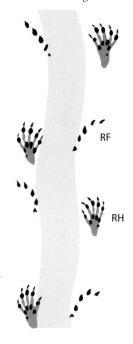

RF

RH

41

The hind foot, which is significantly smaller than the fore foot, has developed normally with five toes, all with long, narrow claws that are clearly visible in the track, and small pads. Moles step on the entire sole of their hind feet. The print is approx. 1.5 cm long and 1.1 cm wide.
Print pattern: When walking, stride length is 3-4 cm and the straddle is wide, widest between the hind feet. On soft ground the animal's underside may leave a trail. When walking fast it has to take two steps with its forepaws for every single step with the hind paws.

Shrew

Individual prints: Shrews are plantigrade and have five claw-bearing toes on both the fore and hind feet. They are very small and light animals, and their footprints are generally so faint and indistinct that it is practi-

cally impossible to distinguish between the tracks of the different species.

Their tracks closely resemble mouse tracks, but you can tell them apart by the fact that the fore print displays five claws while that of the mouse only has four. Tracks can be observed in fine mud by lakeshores, streams and similar spots, but are seen most frequently in snow, where the animals make passages opening onto small circular hollows on the surface. The tracks can usually be seen running from the hollow as a narrow furrow in the snow; at the bottom of this you will find the footprints and a winding trail from the tail.
Print pattern: Individual footprints in the snow vary from 0.5-1 cm in length. Shrews usually move by running or using short jumps. Stride length varies from approx. 3 cm to 5-6 cm depending on the species, and the length of a jump is generally only equivalent to 2-4 times the straddle.

Hare

Individual prints: Hares have five toes on the fore foot, but the inner toe (the thumb) is short and rarely leaves an imprint. The hind foot is long and narrow, with four toes. All the toes have straight, narrow claws, which are clearly visible in the tracks – particularly in snow, where the claw marks can be seen within the limit of the track. On firm ground only the claws will leave marks.

The soles of the feet are covered with a thick layer of strong, springy forward-pointing hair, which has replaced the pads. The layer of hair is particularly well developed under the toes and in clear tracks may produce an imprint resembling pads.

Individual prints have a distinctive

Shrew print pattern and trail in fine mud.

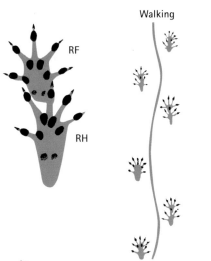

Walking

Hare footprint, showing the imprint from the hair covering the sole.

Hare track. At the top are the two large hind prints side by side, at the bottom the two smaller fore prints.

pointed shape. The fore print on soil is approx. 5 cm long and 3 cm wide, the hind track roughly 6 cm long and 3.5 cm wide. In snow the hind print may be significantly longer, and the width of both fore and hind tracks is greater, as the animal spreads its toes to obtain as large a contact surface as possible. At speed on firm ground hares tread with only the toes of the hind feet, producing prints that are not much larger than the fore prints.

In snow you will often find prints of sitting hares, with their long hind legs side by side, and just in front the small parallel fore prints.

Print pattern: Hare tracks can be recognised first and foremost by the print pattern, which is typical of animals that travel by jumping and galloping. However, a characteristic feature of hare tracks is that the print pattern is very regular and always the same, whether the animal is moving slowly and

Left, track left by hare jumping; right, print of a sitting hare.

43

Distinctive track of a hare in snow. The hare moved from left to right.

steadily or at top speed. In snow, the hind prints will be longer than the fore prints.

Each of the regular print groups is made up of four separate footprints, at the back the two short fore prints, one behind the other almost in a line, and at the front the two hind prints, more side by side and usually longer than the fore prints.

The distance between the individual print groups and between the individual prints in a group increases with the animal's speed of movement, and thus varies greatly. At normal speed it moves at a gallop, but as its speed increases the movement becomes more like jumping.

If you follow a hare track, you will observe that the animal sometimes turns back and follows its own track back a short way

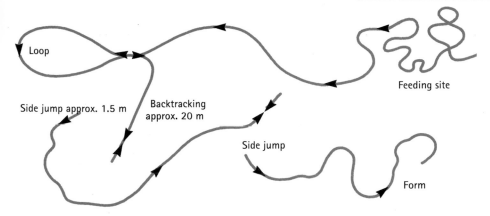

Diagram of the track of a mountain hare's footprints.

before making a huge jump out to the side and continuing in a completely different direction. This strange manoeuvre is undoubtedly intended to confuse and divert any enemies that may be following its trail.

Mountain hare

The mountain hare's track is difficult to distinguish from that of the hare. The individual prints, however, are somewhat broader, as the animal spreads its toes more – especially on the hind feet. In deep loose snow, where a large contact surface is expedient, this will be particularly distinct, and the hind prints here will be very large and pear-shaped.

Rabbit

Individual prints: The print is the same as the hare's but much smaller. On firm ground the hind track is approx. 4 cm long and 2.5 cm wide. You can easily tell the rabbit's tracks from those of the hare just by using an ordinary matchbox: the width of a hare's hind print will be similar to that of the matchbox, whereas a rabbit print will

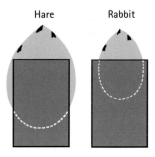

A hare's footprint is the same width as an ordinary matchbox, whereas a rabbit footprint is appreciably narrower than the box.

Rabbit's hind footprint in sand.

45

only be roughly $^2/_3$ of the matchbox's width.
Print pattern: The distance between the
prints in the groups is also much smaller
than for the hare, but in other respects the
print pattern is the same.

Red squirrel

Individual prints: The fore foot has four
long, narrow toes with claws, which are
clearly visible in the track, with the toes
widely splayed. The thumb is fairly small
and leaves no mark, whereas the pad, which
is up near the thumb, generally leaves a distinct mark. The print is approx. 4 cm long
and 2 cm wide.

The hind foot has five toes; the middle
three are long, narrow and roughly equal in
size. These are clearly visible in the track
and very close together. The outer and inner
toes (nos. 1 and 5) are much shorter. They
do not leave such a clear print and are
somewhat turned out. All the toes have
pointed claws that are almost always visible
in the track. The hind print is approx. 5 cm
long and 2.5-3.5 cm wide, depending how
splayed the toes are.

Print pattern: Red squirrels always move by
jumping when on the ground. The tracks
lie close together in very regular jump
groups that bear a certain resemblance to
the hare's, but are of course much smaller.
At the back of the group are the small fore
prints – usually side by side and very close
together. The prints from the large hind feet
will be beside one another just ahead of the
fore prints, slightly further apart and somewhat turned out. The distinctive feature of
squirrel tracks is that they almost always begin and end by a tree.

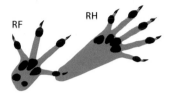

Squirrel print pattern.

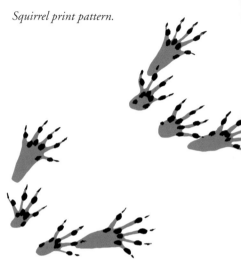

Squirrel's jumping track.

*Squirrel footprints on firm ground in snow.
The large hind prints appear at the front, the
smaller fore prints behind.*

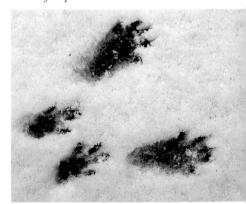

Grey squirrel

The prints and print pattern are difficult to distinguish from those of the red squirrel. However, the heel mark in the hind print is more distinct, and the prints in the jump groups are closer together.

Flying squirrel

The print pattern differs significantly from that of other squirrels: the hind prints are close together and behind the fore prints; the fore prints are side by side and fairly far apart. The animal may move by jumping in an upright position, and the tracks then consist of just hind footprints, positioned close together in pairs.

In snow, clear prints from the 'wing membrane' can be seen, by the fore feet in particular.

Dormouse and hamster

Dormice have five toes on each foot, but the first toe on the fore foot is extremely reduced and leaves no mark. The corresponding toe on the hind foot is also much smaller than the other toes. The track resembles that of the squirrel, but is smaller. The fore print is approx. 2 cm long and 2.2 cm wide, and the hind print approx. 3 cm long and 2.5 cm wide. The claws rarely leave marks, and the prints from the fore foot toe pads form a fainter curve than the squirrel's. The bushy tail often leaves marks on soft ground.

Hamsters have five toes on each foot. The inner toe is reduced and is not visible in the footprints. The toes are long, with claws that show clearly in the track. The fore print is approx. 1.5 cm long and 1 cm wide. The hind print is 2-3.5 cm long and 1 cm wide.

Flying squirrel print pattern (bottom) and trail from four-footed jumping. Note the imprint from the wing membrane by the forefoot.

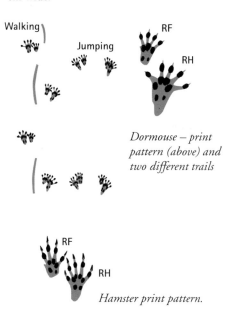

Dormouse – print pattern (above) and two different trails

Hamster print pattern.

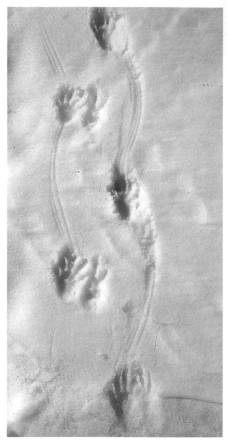

Alpine marmot footprints. At the top are the hind footprints, at the bottom the forefoot prints.

Alpine marmot

Individual prints: The fore foot has four toes. The toe pads are small and oval, and the claws are short and detached. The central pad is large, four-lobed, irregular and almost completely merged. The print is approx. 5 cm long and 3.5 cm wide.

The hind foot has five toes. As on the fore foot, the central pad is large and four-lobed, but is more regular and often not quite as fully merged. It has one or two heel pads. A characteristic of the alpine marmot is that the heel pad is very large and merges with the central pads. The hind print is normally approx. 5.5 cm long and 4 cm wide, but a complete print can be up to 8.5 cm long.

Print pattern: Marmots usually move by walking. The fore and hind prints merge al-

Alpine marmot walking trail. Two track groups are visible (fore and hind feet on top of one another) on the left side and two on the right. The trail between the groups has also been made by the feet, due to the deep snow.

most completely. The footprints are very close to one another in opposite pairs and point straight forward. Stride length is roughly 20 cm.

When jumping, the prints appear together in groups of four, with the fore prints

Beaver footprints on a sandy river bank. On the left is a particularly clear imprint from a forefoot.

Beaver print pattern and trail when walking. Along the centre of the trail is the imprint from its tail (compare photograph on next page).

Walking   Jumping

Alpine marmot, two different trails.

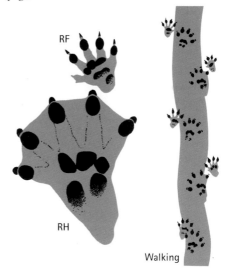

RF

RH

Walking

ahead of the hind prints. The footprints lie close to the central line of the trail and point straight forward. Stride length can be up to 50 cm.

Beaver

Individual prints: The fore foot has five toes with pointed claws, but no webbing. The print often shows only four widely-splayed toes with distinct pointed claw marks. The print is approx. 5.5 cm long and 4.5 cm wide.

49

The hind foot has five toes with blunt claws and webbing between the toes. All the toes and the broad, fat claws are almost always clearly visible in the track, and in soft ground the imprint from the webbing is also distinct. The hind foot is substantially larger than the fore foot, approx. 15 cm long and 10 cm wide.

Print pattern: The beaver's broad tail leaves a trail on soft ground and in snow, and often partially obliterates the footprints. On land beavers normally move by walking.

Tracks from beaver tails across a gravel road with crossing car tracks.

Muskrat

Individual prints: Muskrats have five toes with long pointed claws on both fore and hind feet. However, the inner toe on the fore foot is so small that often the prints of only four toes are visible in the tracks. The length of the fore print is approx. 3.5 cm and the width approx. 3 cm. The hind toes are connected at their bases by a narrow web, and along the edges of the toes are fringes of stiff swimming hairs that make the toe prints wider. The hind print is approx. 7 cm long and 5 cm wide.

Print pattern: The muskrat's long compact tail often leaves a winding trail.

Muskrat print pattern and trail when walking. Imprint from tail is visible.

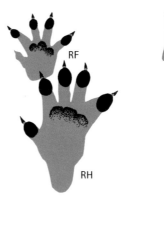

Walking

Coypu

Individual prints: The fore foot has five separate toes (small thumb) and long claws. The hind foot also has five claw-bearing

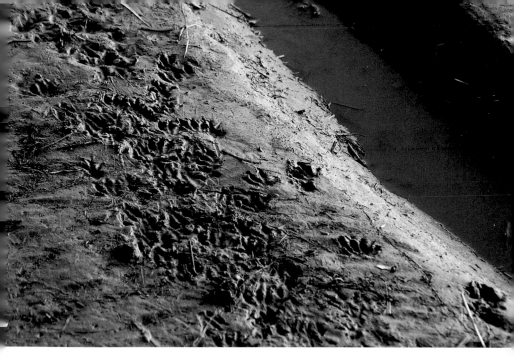

Muskrat footprints.

toes, which are connected by webbing, except the outer toe (no. 5). Toes, claws and pads are normally clearly visible in the track, and on soft ground the imprint of the web can be seen. The hind print is significantly larger than the fore print, but print size varies greatly depending on age and sex. For instance, the proportions between the prints could be: fore foot 6 cm long and 6 cm wide, hind foot 12 cm long, 7 cm wide.

Print pattern: The coypu normally moves by walking, but at greater speeds it can make short jumps. Its long round tail leaves a winding trail, which is usually continuous.

Coypu print pattern and trail when walking. Imprint from tail is visible.

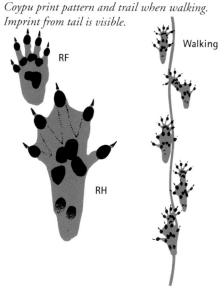

RF

RH

Walking

Norway lemming is rarely seen above the snow in winter. Below, its path through a thinner layer of snow.

Small rodents, mice, voles and rats

The common characteristic of these animals is that the fore foot has four well--developed claw-bearing toes that appear widely splayed in the track. The hind foot has five claw-bearing toes; the outer two are short and positioned a long way back on the foot, whereas the central three are long and thin. In the track the outer toes are widely splayed, while the imprint from the middle toes is more together and pointing forward. As with other rodents, the fore feet are significantly larger than the hind feet.

These are almost exclusively small, light animals whose footprints are usually faint and indistinct. Therefore in practice it is almost always impossible to distinguish between the various different species on the basis of the footprints alone. So for identification you must pay attention to other signs such as feeding signs and droppings. The habitat in which the track is found can also act as an excellent guide. As most small rodents live concealed in vegetation, it is only really on snow that you come across their tracks. With species that live by water or in dunes, however, tracks may also be seen in mud or wet sand. Rat and house mouse tracks can be observed in the dust on floors of mills, granaries and other similar places.

Lemming: The hind print is 17-19 mm and its trail is distinctive as it swings from side to side over longer distances (length of swing up to 36 m).

Vole: Voles are short-legged and have relatively short tails. They are more stockily built than mice and generally move more slowly and heavily. There is often a clear size difference between the hind and fore print but not as marked as in mice.

Voles usually move by walking. Some species jump fairly frequently, but trotting seldom occurs. Print size varies from species to species; the *water vole's* hind print is 20-25 mm, the *field vole's* 17-18 mm and the *bank vole's* 16-17 mm long.

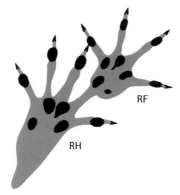

RF

RH

Water vole print pattern on soft ground.

Water vole track in mud.
Both fore and hind footprints visible.

Tracks of field vole jumping in snow. Note marks from the long tail between the tracks.

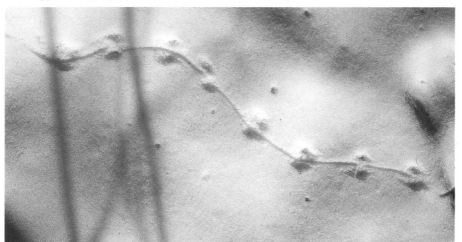

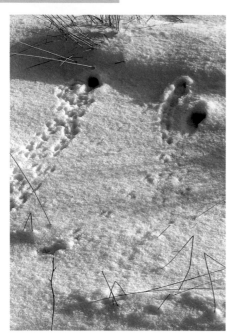

Mouse: Mice have a lighter build, long tails, and their legs – particularly the hind legs – are long and suitable for jumping. Among wood mice and yellow-necked mice jumping is the most commonly used gait, while rats and house mice just as frequently use walking. In snow, where you most often see jumping tracks, the four prints appear close together in groups, with a clear size difference between the fore and hind tracks, and generally also a distinct imprint from the long tail. Hind print lengths are: *brown rat* 30-45 mm, *house mouse* 12-14 mm, *striped field mouse* 16-18 mm, *wood mouse* 20-21 mm, and *yellow-necked mouse* 22-24 mm.

Brown rat tracks around entrance hole.

Field vole. Numerous walking prints can be seen to and from the holes leading down to the vole's tunnels under the snow.

Brown rat walking track, and print detail (bottom).

Walking

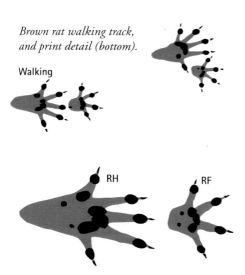

RH   RF

RF

RH

Genet print pattern.

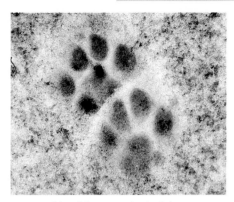

Fore and hind footprints (top) of domestic cat in melting snow.

Genet

Individual prints: The tracks may resemble those of the fox, but are not as large (rarely larger than 4 x 4 cm) and less oblong. The central pad is often triangular with three faint lobe marks. There are four relatively small toe pads, and imprints from the claws are often clearly visible. It differs in this way from a cat's track, with which it can also be confused.

Domestic cat

Individual prints: Domestic cats are digitigrade; they have five toes on the fore foot and four on the hind foot. However, the inner toe on the fore foot is so high up that it does not leave an imprint. There are four well-developed toe pads and a large three-lobed central pad. The claws are long, pointed and elevated, so they do not touch the ground when walking. The print is distinctive due to its almost circular outline, sharply-defined pads and lack of claw marks. A medium-sized cat's footprint is roughly 3-3.5 cm long and 3 cm wide.
Print pattern: When walking on firm

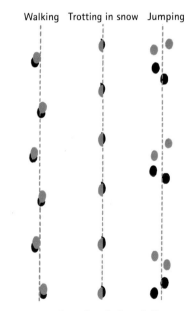

Walking Trotting in snow Jumping

Domestic cat's trail with three different gaits.

ground the hind foot is normally placed ahead of the fore print; in snow it is placed on top of the fore print. Stride length is approx. 30cm and the straddle is distinct.

When trotting, the hind foot is placed in the fore print and the stride length increases to 35-40 cm. The straddle is so narrow that the tracks are almost in a line. A cat's trotting track thus closely resembles that of a fox in snow, but can be easily distinguished from this by the small size of the track and the much shorter stride length.

When fleeing, cats move using jumps of varying lengths.

Wild cat

The print and print pattern are very similar to that of the domestic cat. However, the individual print is larger and comparatively longer, approx. 4 cm long and 3.5 cm wide.

Lynx

Individual prints: The individual print is like a cat's, but roughly three times as large. The fore print measures approx. 6.5 cm in length and 5.5 cm in width, the hind print approx. 7.5 cm and 6 cm respectively.

Print pattern: The lynx moves mainly by walking or at a slow gallop. In both cases the hind foot is normally placed in the fore print, and the straddle is so small that the tracks are almost in a line. With very slow walking, however, the hind foot is placed ahead of the fore print, and the straddle is evident. In normal walking the stride length is approx. 80 cm; when trotting this can increase to 135 cm. When fleeing it usually gallops, with a stride length of approx. 150 cm; when jumping, it can be as much as 7 m.

The tracks of lynx and wolf are often mixed up. The lynx track is asymmetrical, looking like a hand without a thumb. Right-hand paws (both front- and hind paws) have 'the middle finger' as the longest, then 'the ring finger', then 'the index finger' etc.

With the wolf track the two middle toes are of the same length. If you follow a lynx track, this field characteristic is easy to recognize, as is the symmetrical track of a wolf.

Tracks of a walking lynx. You can glimpse middle toes of varying length – an important detail when identifying lynx tracks from wolf tracks.

Print from lynx's forefoot.

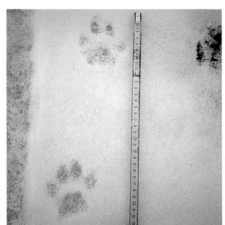

Beech marten and pine marten

Individual prints: They have five claw-bearing toes on each foot, which all leave an imprint in clear tracks. In many instances, however, the print from the inner toe is barely visible. The claws almost always leave a clear print.

In addition to the toe pads, there are four small middle pads positioned in a semi-circle, but these only appear as three close-set, roundish depressions in the print. The fore foot also has a small, round carpal pad, behind the middle pads at the outer edge of the foot. As they tread with their entire fore foot sole, which is fairly short, prints from the carpal pads are often visible in clear tracks and are an excellent distinctive feature of the fore print.

Beech marten and pine marten tracks are virtually identical and very difficult to tell apart. However, the *pine marten's* track is slightly larger and bolder than the beech marten's, and the outlines of the print appear more indistinct. The latter is due to the covering of hair on the sole between the pads, which grows so vigorously, especially in winter, that it completely covers the pads. The pine marten's fore print is roughly 4 cm long and 3.7 cm wide; the hind print is 4.5 cm and 3.5 cm respectively.

In contrast, the pads are usually fairly clear to see in *beech marten* tracks. On firm ground its fore print is approx. 3.5 cm long and 3.2 cm wide, the hind print is approx. 4 cm and 3 cm respectively.

In loose snow both species' prints can be surprisingly large – often twice as large as usual.

Print pattern: The stride length is generally relatively short. Jumping is by far the pre-

Typical trail of pine marten, showing paired prints.

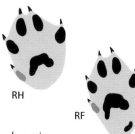

Prints of marten (beech or pine marten) fore and hind foot.

57

ferred gait, and martens use this in most circumstances, but sometimes they move by walking or trotting, usually placing the hind foot behind the fore print.

Jump groups are very distinctive and characteristic in most members of the marten family. Individual prints in the track groups are always very close together, and generally either one or both of the hind tracks will be on top of the fore prints, thus producing 'triple tracks' or 'paired tracks'. If you follow a series of track groups, you will

Marten (beech or pine marten) trail for three different gaits.

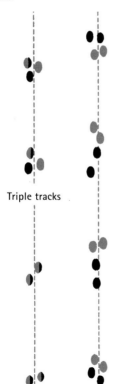

Triple tracks

Paired tracks   Jumping

see that the print pattern of any individual constantly varies; you will rarely find two jump groups that are identical. Paired tracks appear most often in snow, with the two prints close together side by side, often slightly angled. Stride length varies from approx. 40 cm up to around 1 m.

Polecat

Individual prints: Its print greatly resembles the beech marten's, but is smaller (it is roughly midway between the beech marten's and the stoat's in size, see page 57). On reasonably firm ground the length of the fore print is 3-3.5 cm, width 2.5-4 cm depending on the spread of the toes. On soft ground and in snow, where it steps on a

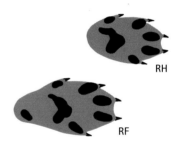

RH

RF

Print of polecat fore and hind foot.

Track group of polecat, showing tail mark by one footprint.

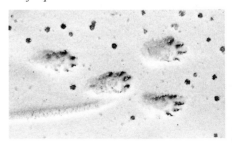

larger area of sole, the hind print can be 4-4.5 cm long. As the covering of hair between the pads is short, the prints from the pads and claws will generally be clearly visible.

Print pattern: Its print pattern is the same as the marten; however, in jump groups you will quite often see four separate footprints. Stride length varies; on firm ground it is around 50-60 cm, in loose snow 35-50 cm.

Mink

Its print resembles that of polecat in shape and size, and it is practically impossible to distinguish between the two. Mink perhaps have a tendency to splay their toes less than polecats, and in terms of print pattern the distance between jump groups appears more constant.

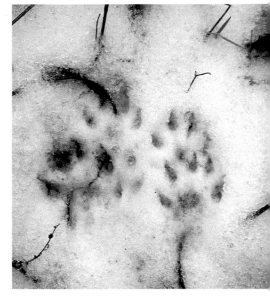

Mink footprints in snow.

Mink trail with paired tracks.

Stoat

Individual prints: Stoats have a typical small marten foot (see beech marten), but due to their size and light weight their tracks are often fairly indistinct. In addition, the pads are covered by hair in winter. Only on very soft ground will you see clear prints showing five splayed toes with claws and the middle pads, which produce three small, round depressions, forming an approximate right angle pointing forwards.

Stoat prints are recognisable primarily by

Stoat track in deep snow; imprints of both the feet and the body visible.

their size combined with the characteristic marten jumps (see beech marten, previous column). The fore print is approx. 2 cm long and 1.5 cm wide, the hind print approx. 3.5 cm and 1.3 cm respectively.

Print pattern: Walking prints are very rare, as they move almost exclusively by jumping. On reasonably hard ground, such as solid snow, the tracks in jump groups may be four and four, often similar to a small hare track. In loose snow triple prints and especially paired prints are most common. The distance between jump groups varies greatly. It is often fairly constant over long stretches, around 40 cm, but just as frequently you will see regular alternation between long and short jumps, e.g. 70 cm and 30 cm.

If you follow a stoat track in snow, you will often see that when hunting small rodents the stoat suddenly burrows down through the snow, creating a tunnel that opens out on the surface of the snow a little way off.

Print from stoat fore and hind foot.

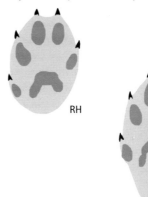

RH

RF

Otter prints in sand.

Weasel prints around the entrance to its hole.

Otter

Individual prints: Otters have five toes on each foot connected by webbing. Their tracks are very distinctive and easy to recognise.

Otter slide on snow-covered slope.

Weasel and least weasel

The print and print pattern of the weasel and least weasel (the latter a northern European subspecies) are identical and closely resemble the stoat's.

Individual prints: The print greatly resembles the stoat's, but is smaller, approx. 1.4 cm long and 1 cm wide. They do not travel on the surface of the snow as much as stoats; holes and snow tunnels are very common. When a weasel catches a mouse, it will carry it back to its den (stockpiles), holding the mouse crosswise in its mouth, and in snow this will leave an imprint by each pair of footprints.

Print pattern: The print pattern also closely resembles the stoat's; the distance between jump groups again alternates between short and long jumps.

Otters leave paired prints in deep snow. The picture also shows a furrow made by its body.

The fore footprint is almost circular, 6.5-7 cm long and approx. 6 cm wide. The print from the thumb is only visible in very clear tracks, and the webbing generally only leaves distinct marks in soft snow. The claw marks are very small and appear as small points on the toe pad imprints.

The hind print is longer than the fore print and varies in length from approx. 6 cm to 9 cm, depending how much of its sole the otter steps on; however, you often

Otter print pattern.

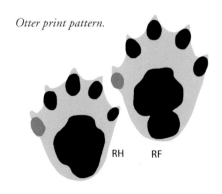

RH   RF

see prints of the entire sole. Imprints from the claws and web are as for the fore foot. **Print pattern:** When walking, which is rare, the hind foot is placed behind the fore print and the straddle is wide. When trotting, also fairly rare, the hind track more or less covers the fore print, and the stride length is around 70-80 cm.

Jumping is the otter's usual gait, characterised by extremely large variations in the position of the individual prints in jump groups. A particularly distinctive print pattern occurs when all four footprints appear in a diagonal line. In snow, paired prints are common, and in deep, loose snow, due to

the otter's short legs, its body will create a furrow, with paired tracks at the bottom at relatively short intervals, and its tail often leaving a trail. Normal, steady jumps are approx. 40-45 cm in length.

An interesting and not uncommon track is the broad, long furrow made by otters sliding down snow slopes on their bellies. When playing they use suitable slopes as regular slides.

Badger

Individual prints: Badgers are typical plantigrades with five toes with long claws on each foot. As they tread heavily, the details of the prints are usually clearly visible, and since the shape is also distinctive, resembling a fairly small bear print, badger prints are always easy to recognise.

The print shows the five toe pads close together almost in a row. The imprint of

Otter's trail for three different gaits.

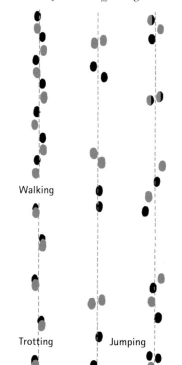

Walking

Trotting   Jumping

Print from a badger's forefoot with hind footprint on top slightly further back.

63

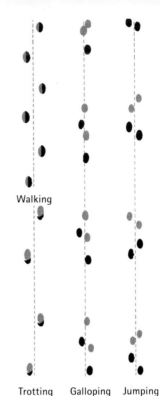

Walking

Trotting   Galloping   Jumping

Badger trail.

Badger's trail for three different gaits.

the inner toe, however, is often faint or missing completely. The large, slightly lobed central pad and the claws are always visible – the very long fore foot claws, in particular, leave distinct marks, which may extend several centimetres in front of the toe pads. The hind foot claws are much shorter.

Badgers normally only tread with the front part of the fore foot, producing a print approx. 4 cm wide and 5 cm long; if the entire foot is used the length is approx. 7 cm.

The hind print is more often an imprint

of the entire foot; the width is approx. 3.5 cm, length to back edge of central pad approx. 4.5 cm, to heel approx. 6.5 cm.
Print pattern: Badgers usually move by walking, often placing the hind foot in the fore print. Stride length is approx. 50 cm and the straddle is very distinct. When covering longer distances, they trot. On firm ground the hind foot is then placed ahead of the fore print, and stride length is around 70-80 cm. When moving rapidly across open stretches, or when frightened, they will gallop or trot.

Wolverine

Individual prints: Wolverines are only partially plantigrade, and their tracks often have imprints of the front part of the foot only. They have five toes with fairly powerful claws on each foot, and the five toe pads and two carpal pads on the fore foot, are generally clearly visible. The middle pads are less sharply defined due to the thick hair on the sole of the foot, and there may be no claw marks at all. If the inner toe print is indistinct or completely missing, the track can be confused with a wolf track (see page 71), particularly in snow. However, the print pattern is especially distinct: the wolverine's gait is often quite different (i.e. jumping – see right), and the

Wolverine prints from jumping in firm snow. Only the front part of the foot is visible.

Wolverine in its favourite habitat with its legs in the air.

Typical wolverine trail – with footprints in groups of three.

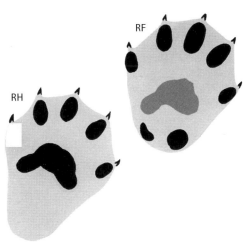

RF

RH

Print of wolverine fore and hind feet.

tracks from its fore and hind feet are placed behind one another when walking. The fore print is 14-18 cm long and 10-13 cm wide, while the hind print appears shorter, as the heel pad rarely leaves an imprint.

Print pattern: Wolverines move primarily by jumping, like their close relatives the martens, with variations in print pattern that are very distinctive (see page 58). So in snow, paired tracks are most common. They also trot quite often, but walking tracks are very rare.

Fox

Individual prints: Foxes are digitigrade, with five toes on the fore foot and four on the hind. However, prints from both fore and hind feet show only four toes, as the inner toe of the fore foot is so high up. They have four well-developed toe pads and a large central pad. Their claws are long, thin and pointed. The print, which has clear imprints from the pads and claws, is so symmetrical that it is generally not possible to determine from an individual print whether it comes from a right or left foot. The fore print is somewhat larger than the hind print, but otherwise they are almost identical. The length is approx. 5 cm, width 4-4.5 cm.

Fox tracks can easily be confused with dog tracks of the same size. However, fox pads are smaller and not as close together. In addition, the fox's two central toe pads are further forward, leaving a relatively large space between their back edge and the front edge of the central pad. If you draw a line across the front edges of the outer toe

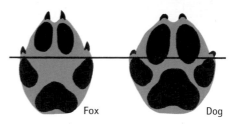

Fox   Dog

Fox and dog prints can easily be confused, but, as shown here, there is a clear difference in the position of the pads.

pads, it will be behind or just touching the back edges of the two central toe pads, whereas in dogs it would be in front of this back edge. Compared with dog prints, fox prints also appear longer and more delicate, and the claw marks are thinner and more pointed.

In winter – particularly in northern areas – the hair between the pads can grow so vigorously that it covers them. The prints are then larger, rounder and have blurred outlines.

Print pattern: Foxes use all types of gait, but move most frequently by trotting.

Print of a large dog in wet sand.

Print of fox, made in wet clay that has subsequently dried.

Print of wolf, made in wet clay that has subsequently dried.

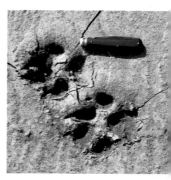

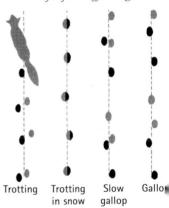

Fox trotting tracks in deep snow.

Fox's trail for four different gaits.

| Trotting | Trotting in snow | Slow gallop | Gallop |

Fox trotting tracks on firm ground, snow-covered ice.

On firm ground foxes' trotting tracks differ somewhat from the normal dog or wolf pattern, as they appear as a row of oblique print pairs, consisting of a fore print and in front, a hind track diagonally to one side. All the hind prints are on the same side. This curious print pattern occurs because the fox trots with its body positioned diagonally. Sometimes it may switch and swing its rear body over to the other side. In snow or on soft ground, however, it will al-ways keep its body straight in the direction of movement and place its hind foot exactly in the fore print.

Stride length when trotting is around 70-80 cm.

When walking on firm ground it usually places its hind foot ahead of the fore print. Stride length is 25-30 cm. If frightened or being chased, it will jump or gallop, using extremely varied stride lengths.

Arctic fox

Its print is like the fox's, but somewhat smaller, and in winter blurred and rounder due to the thick hair on its soles. The print pattern is the same as the fox, but the stride length is shorter for all gaits. It trots less than the fox, but gallops much more often.

Dog

The print and print pattern are like the fox's, and footprints of the same size can be confused (photo p. 67). However, dog prints appear more compact, as the pads are larger and closer together. The central pad extends almost up to the middle toe pads, and if you draw a line across the front edge of the outer toe pads, it will generally inter-sect the middle toe pads, see page 67. The claw marks are thick and stumpy. The fore print is much larger than the hind print, and the rear edge of the central pad curves inward, whereas on the hind foot it curves outward.

Wolf

The print and print pattern resemble a large dog's, and the two can be confused very eas-ily. However, a wolf's toe pads are longer and not as close together, so the splaying between the two middle toes is somewhat greater than with dogs. The claw marks are also more pronounced, being longer and more pointed than in a dog. The fore print of an adult wolf is approx. 11 cm long and 10 cm wide, the hind print approx. 8 cm long and 7 cm wide.

When walking, which is relatively rare, the stride length is 80-90 cm; when trot-

Prints from a wolf's four paws; hind prints on the left, fore prints on the right.

ting, by far the most common gait, stride length is around 1 m, when jumping or galloping, 1.5 m or more.

Raccoon dog

Raccoon dog tracks can resemble fox tracks, but the toes are more widely splayed, so the prints from the toe pads appear as a spread fan ahead of the central pad print, rather than together like those of a fox. The toe pads and claws are generally clearly visible. The fore print is 4-5 cm long and 5-6 cm wide, while the hind print is slightly smaller. The prints are never in a line – as is often seen with foxes – but have a wobbly, irregular course.

Wolf track in deep snow.

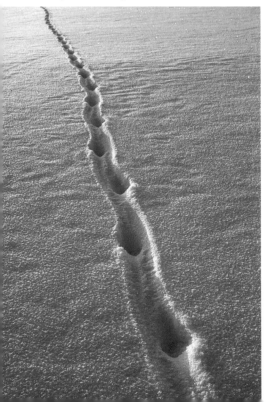

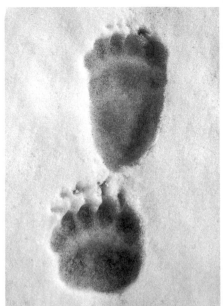

Bear footprints, hind foot at the top and forefoot below.

Bear

Individual prints: Bears are plantigrade and have five toes with long claws on each foot. Prints from the large toe pads appear side by side, and marks from the claws are generally distinct. A well-defined ridge of compressed material appears between the toe pad and central pad imprints.

The fore print is short and broad, as bears mainly step on the foremost part of the foot, and only in very clear tracks is the entire sole visible. Print size varies greatly according to age; with a full-grown bear the length is approx. 28 cm, width approx. 21 cm.

The hind print, which often shows the

movement. The straddle is large, and the stride length, which varies greatly, is approx. 150 cm for a fully-grown animal. When trotting, the straddle is narrower and tracks are more forward-pointing. The hind foot is placed in, or close to, the fore print. They seldom bound and then only over short distances. However, in very deep snow they generally use this gait.

Raccoon

Raccoons were introduced to Germany from North America as fur-bearing animals. They are plantigrade and have five long toes with large claws on both fore and hind feet. Their track resembles a bear's, but much smaller. The fore print is approx. 7 cm long and equally broad, with widely-splayed toes. The hind print, with the toes closer together, is approx. 9 cm long and 6-7 cm wide. Their footprints often appear in pairs, e.g. left hind foot beside right fore foot (compare fox tracks, page 67).

Bear trail on a sandbank by a river.

entire sole, bears a certain resemblance to a print from a very large, naked human foot, but toe no. 1, equivalent to our big toe, is the smallest and shortest in bears. A hind print from a full-grown bear is approx. 30 cm long and 17 cm wide.

Print pattern: Bears normally move by walking, placing the hind foot well ahead of the fore print. Tracks are generally roughly diagonal in relation to the direction of

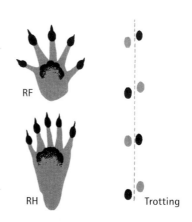

Raccoon print pattern and trail when trotting.

71

Seal tracks on a sandbank. Alongside the trail made by the body are marks from the flippers.

Seal

Seal tracks can be found on mud and sandbanks or snow-covered ice. They are very distinctive and cannot be confused with any other animal track. When moving, the body is hardly lifted, but is propelled forward using the front flippers; for rapid movement, e.g. when fleeing, the hind flippers must also be used to push it forward. So the track consists of a broad trail made by the body, and at each side – in pairs – a series of imprints from the front flippers, with the five claws usually clearly visible, in a line parallel with the direction of movement.

Seal trail. See also plate, page 19.

Cloven-hoofed animals

For further information on cloven-hoof tracks, see page 31.

Wild boar

Individual prints: Unlike most deer tracks, wild boar tracks are distinctive, as the dew claws usually leave clear marks whatever gait is used. However, with fairly young animals, imprints from the dew claws may be faint or missing completely. Imprints from the dew claws appear some way out to the sides, making the print outline trapezoid, whereas deer's dew claws leave an imprint just behind the forehoof prints, so the entire print forms a rectangle. In snow, when the print is often just a hole with no detail, you can therefore tell the two apart, as the wild boar print is widest at the back.

Size varies greatly depending on age and sex. The width of a good-sized animal's forehoof print will be around 6-7 cm. Young animals' hoofs are pointed at the front, while in older animals they are distinctly rounded and plump.

Print pattern: When walking and trotting individual prints are somewhat turned out, and the hind foot is usually placed exactly in the fore print. However, in some cases the hind print will be dislocated slightly in relation to the fore print, leaving two pairs of dew claw imprints just behind one another. Stride length when walking is approx. 80 cm for an adult. With rapid galloping or bounding the prints appear individually in groups of four, with the cleaves widely splayed.

Wild boar print in mud. Bottom left is a clear imprint from the dew claw.

Wild boar trail when walking and bounding.

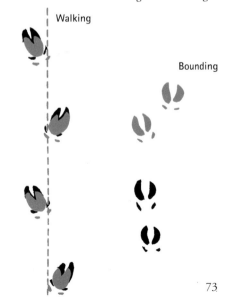

Walking

Bounding

73

Domestic pig

The tracks are essentially the same as those of wild boar. However, shape and size varies somewhat depending on the breed, and the state of wear of the cleaves.

Red deer

Individual prints: Red deer prints are relatively broad, and the outer edges of the cleaves curve evenly towards the tip. The forehooves in particular are extremely rounded and the track from a large animal may resemble the imprint from a boot heel seen from in front. In clear tracks the pad imprint can be seen behind as a rounded depression, forming approx. one third of the

print length, and going up in front slightly in keeping with the curved sole. A full-grown red deer stag's fore print is 8-9 cm long and 6-7 cm wide, while the hind print is smaller, 6-7 cm long and 4-5 cm wide.

Print pattern: When walking or steady trotting, the most common gaits for undisturbed animals, the hind foot is placed in or close to the fore print. The dew claws do

Red deer trotting track in sand.

Red deer stag footprints, at the top the forefoot and below the hind foot.

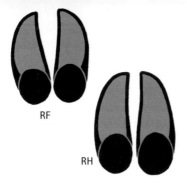

Red deer fore and hind prints.
Below, red deer trail for three different gaits.

not normally leave marks, and the straddle is relatively narrow in hinds and youngsters, but distinct with stags. Stride length for an adult varies between 80 and 150 cm. When trotting fast on firm ground the hind foot is placed ahead of the fore print – the greater the speed, the further ahead. The straddle is also reduced and the cleaves widely splayed; imprints from the dew claws are usually also visible. Stride length varies greatly with trotting speed and can be up to approx. 350 cm. When fleeing, galloping or jumping is common, leaving prints with widely splayed cleaves and distinct imprints from the dew claws.

Fallow deer

Individual prints: Fallow deer have narrower and longer prints than red deer. The cleave imprints are often very pointed with almost parallel outer edges at the back. The pad imprint, which makes up almost half the track's length, is often clearly marked.

Fallow deer fore and hind prints.

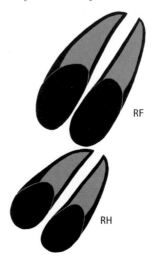

Trotting | Galloping | Jumping

RF
RH

RH

RF

75

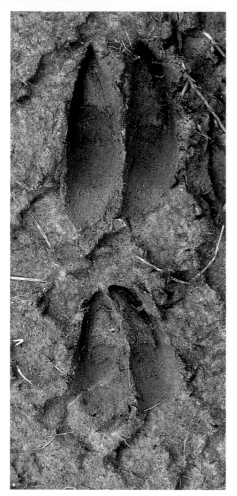

Sika deer

Their track closely resembles the fallow deer's, but is broader, and the straddle is wider.

Muntjac

The muntjac lives in Southeast Asia, from where it was introduced to France and England. Its prints are easily recognised by their very small size, usually under 3 cm long, and there is a tendency for the inner cleave to be less developed than the outer. However, in many animals the cleaves are symmetrical. The dew claws are small and normally only leave imprints on very soft ground, and when the animal jumps.

The asymmetrical print of the muntjac's foot.

White-tailed deer

The white-tailed or Virginia deer is from North America and was introduced into Finland, from where it is spreading. It occasionally turns up as an escape from collec-

Fallow deer footprints – at the top the forefoot and below the hind foot.

White-tailed deer fore and hind prints; note that the distance between the hoofs and the dew claws is greater in the hind print.

Doe prints are 5-6 cm long and 3.5-4 cm wide, while those of the buck can be up to 8 cm long and 5 cm wide.

Print pattern: Print patterns for the various gaits are as for red deer, but stride length is somewhat shorter.

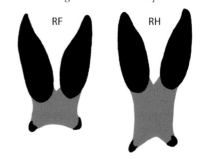

RF   RH

tions. Its print, which is approx. 7 cm long, may resemble that of fallow deer.

Roe deer

Individual prints: Distinctive, due to its small size, the cleaves' narrow, pointed shape and the fact that it is level at the bottom, as the pad extends right out to the cleave tip. However, the cleave tips of older animals are often plump. The print is approx. 4.5 cm

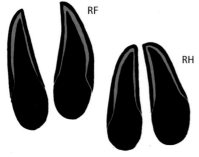

Roe deer fore and hind prints.

Roe deer fore print from jumping in sand. The hoofs are splayed, and clear marks are visible from the dew claws.

In deep snow the roe deer lifts its feet and swings them forward, and this is clearly visible in its trail.

long and 3 cm wide. No clear difference in the size of the buck and the doe prints.

Print pattern: Roe deer mostly walk, and the straddle is generally narrow, although it may vary. The tracks are somewhat turned out, and the dew claws do not leave marks. Stride length is 60-90 cm, and the hind foot is normally placed in the fore print. The forecleaves are usually slightly splayed; the rear cleaves appear close together.

When trotting, the prints appear almost in a line, with the individual prints pointing forward. With steady trotting, the hind foot is placed in the fore print, but as speed increases it is placed further and further ahead of the fore print. The forecleaves are often very widely splayed when trotting, and stride length is usually 100-140cm.

When fleeing the animal will jump or gallop. In these tracks imprints from the

Roe deer trail in deep snow.

dew claws are generally visible, almost transverse in the fore print, but more parallel in the hind print.

In jump tracks the cleaves are always splayed; the forecleaves in a very pronounced V-shape, the rear cleaves much less. Jump length is generally around 2 m, but varies greatly and may be up to twice that.

Elk

Individual prints: Due to their size elk tracks can only be confused with those of domestic cattle, but elks have long, pointed cleaves that leave an almost rectangular track, while cattle cleaves are less pointed and much rounder in shape. Elk tracks also often have dew claw imprints, especially the fore print, which is seldom the case with cattle. As with roe deer, the pad extends right out to the tip of the cleave.

Elk footprint; note the imprint from the dew claws.

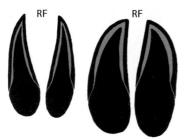

Print size varies greatly depending on sex and age, and older animals' cleave tips are generally blunter than those of younger animals. A full-grown elk bull's fore print is 13-15 cm long and 11-13 cm wide, while the hind print is 14-15.5 cm and 10.5-11 cm respectively. The female's print is smaller than the male's.

Elk- print from forefoot of calf (left) and adult bull (right).

Elk trail in deep snow.

Print pattern: Elk usually walk or trot. They seldom gallop and then only over short stretches – usually only young animals. The straddle when walking is very distinct.

Reindeer

Individual prints: Reindeer tracks are very distinctive and easy to recognise by the crescent-shaped cleave that produces an almost circular imprint with sharply-defined edges. The dew claws are large and positioned low; they leave marks even when the animal is moving at a steady walk. The fore print from a good-sized bull is approx. 8.5 cm long and 10 cm wide, the hind print approx. 8.5 cm long and 9.5 cm wide. The female's print is generally more pointed and slightly smaller.

Print pattern: Reindeer usually walk or trot, galloping and jumping are rare. When walking, the straddle is distinct, the tracks turned out and stride length can be 100-120 cm. When trotting, stride length can be 130-150 cm.

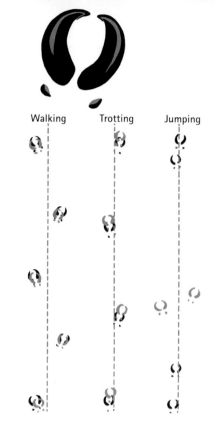

Walking   Trotting   Jumping

Reindeer prints with dew claw marks (top) and trails for three different gaits.

Reindeer footprints with clear dew claw prints.

Mouflon

Individual prints: Mouflon have long, slender cleaves that do not merge completely even on compression of the tips. Besides the elongated shape, the track is distinctive in that the cleave tips are almost always splayed, even at a steady walk, and quite distinctly angular at the back. The dew claws never leave marks, even when jumping. A full-grown ram's print is approx. 5.5cm long

Comparison of mouflon, domestic sheep and roe deer prints.

and 4.4 cm wide. The ewe's print is slightly shorter and narrower.

Print pattern: Mouflon usually walk or trot, but when fleeing they gallop or jump. The straddle is generally large, but stride length is relatively short.

Print from a mouflon's long, slender hoof.

Domestic sheep hoofprints on soft ground.

Domestic sheep

Domestic sheep prints can resemble roe deer's, but are broader and more rectangular, with distinct, rounded cleave tips. The dew claws are so high up that they never leave marks. The size varies according to age and breed, but for an adult is usually around 5-6 cm long and 4-5 cm wide.

Chamois

Individual prints: Chamois live in the mountains, and their hooves have adapted in various ways to moving about on crags and steep slopes. They tread only on the

81

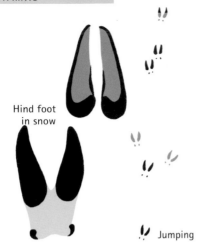

Hind foot
in snow

Jumping

Chamois print pattern and trail in snow.

and there is always – even at the back – a large, clear gap between the cleaves. The track from a full-grown animal is approx. 6 cm long and 3.5 cm wide.

Print pattern: A walking track is rectangular, almost square, but at faster gaits it becomes more trapezoid due to the greater splaying of the cleave tips. In flight tracks the dew claws are a long way back, approx. 10 cm behind the back edge of the cleaves. This is because the animal's legs give way so much when landing that the dew claws touch the ground.

Domestic goat hoofprint on wet ground.

edge of the hoof, which is very well developed and composed of a resilient, rubbery material. In addition, the mobility between the foot's two large digits is relatively great. Due to the animal's habitat – stony slopes, crags etc. – opportunities to observe their tracks occur mainly in winter. The dew claws are high up and only leave marks in flight tracks and in sufficiently deep snow.

The individual prints are very distinctive in shape. The two cleave prints are angular and roughly equally wide at front and back,

Prints from domestic goat, domestic cattle and horse (with and without shoe).

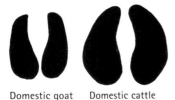
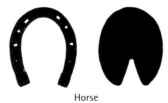

Domestic goat   Domestic cattle   Horse

Domestic goat

Goat hooves are rounded at the ends and narrower at the front than the back. The cleave tips are often fairly widely splayed, and the individual cleave is convex on the outside and concave on the inside. The dew claws do not leave marks. Print size varies somewhat from breed to breed.

Musk ox

Individual prints: The print is 8-10 cm long and the print kidney-shaped and rounded. Prints from the dew claws are

Musk ox trail in sand.

Domestic cattle prints are seldom confused with others, as they appear in places where it is easy to guess what animal has been there.

sometimes visible just behind the hoof print. It can resemble a reindeer print. **Print pattern:** A musk ox's stride length is approx. 1 m and the straddle is wide – wider than a reindeer.

Domestic cattle

Prints vary greatly in shape and size depending on the condition of the hoof. The individual cleave is rounded and broad in proportion to its length. On the outside it is convex, while the inner edge is concave at the front and convex at the back. The dew claws do not normally leave a print. Print size varies greatly from breed to breed, but may be 10-12 cm long and 9-10 cm wide. See also page 78 for the difference between domestic cattle and elk tracks.

Hoofed animals

For further information on non-cloven hoof structure, see page 32.

Horse's hoof with shoe.

Horse's hoof without shoe.

Horse

Horse prints can be found in two forms: with and without shoes. If the animal is wearing shoes, only the imprint of the actual shoe is visible, and identification is easy. Without shoes the hoof leaves a large almost circular imprint with a deep notch at the back. Print size varies greatly depending on breed.

Donkey

Donkey tracks resemble those of a small horse.

Bird footprints

Foot structure

When a bird moves on the ground, it only treads on its toes, as the midfoot – the 'shank' – that makes up the long section of the leg nearest the foot never touches the ground when walking. The portion after the foot therefore corresponds to the heel, and not, as you might think, the knee (see diagram below).

A bird's foot never has more than four toes. Of these, three are generally pointed forward, while the fourth is turned backwards. Compared with a mammal's foot (see page 29) it is toe no. 5 that has disappeared and toe no. 1 (the thumb) that is turned backwards. Of the forward-pointing toes, the middle toe (no. 3) is usually the longest. The rear toe can be large, but is often small and may be so high up that it does not leave prints. In some birds the rear toe is missing completely.

In certain birds, e.g. grouse, the plumage extends right out onto the toes, but in most the upperside of the toes is covered with horny scales, while the undersides are covered with horny papillae for protection against wear and cold. On the outermost joint of each toe is a claw; in birds of prey it is large and powerful, while in ducks for example it is shorter.

The shape of the foot, which is reflected in the footprint, varies greatly and tells us

something about the different species' habitats and way of life, and sometimes also about what they eat. In aquatic birds the foot's surface is often increased by webbing, a horny fold of skin that in ducks and gulls links the three forward-pointing toes, and in cormorants links all four toes. In coots and grebes each individual toe has a border of

Typical structure of a bird's foot compared with a mammal's foot. The two bones shown in the bird's leg are the bottom shank consisting of fused tarsal and metatarsal bones (the tarsometatarsus), and at the top the tibiotarsus. The joint, which is often mistaken for the knee, is in fact the heel (ankle).

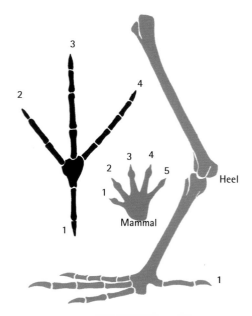

webbing. Waders have long, slender toes that are widely splayed and therefore suitable for walking on soft ground without sinking. Gamebirds' feet are short and powerful, suitable for running, and perching birds have a long rear toe that can flex in towards the front toes for a firm grip around branches.

Types of prints

When birds move on the ground they either hop, walk or run. When hopping, the prints appear in pairs, while walking prints appear in a zigzag, or sometimes in a line. When running, stride length is longer and the straddle (distance between right and left footprint) narrower than when walking.

Bird tracks are generally only seen on fairly soft ground, e.g. along muddy shores, in wet sand or in snow. In snow you will often also be able to observe imprints from the wing feathers at places where they took off, whereas there will generally only be an imprint from the body where they landed. With pheasants, you will often also be able

Wing marks from bird taking off.

to see imprints from the long tail feathers when landing in snow.

Proper species identification for bird tracks is often extremely difficult due to the huge range of possibilities – it requires experience and extensive knowledge of birds. When trying to identify a bird print, take note of its size first and foremost; the length of the middle toe and the length and shape of the rear toe – if present – are of particular significance. You should also note the size of the angle between the outer toes, and whether the toes are long and slender or short and powerful. Any imprint from webbing is naturally also an important characteristic.

Comparison of grey heron, stork and crane prints, which can be distinguished by the hind toe shape.

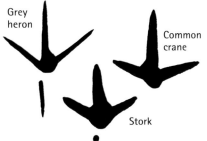

Grey heron

Common crane

Stork

Gamebirds

Gamebirds spend much of their time on the ground, which is where they have their nests, and where they mostly hunt for food. So you will often find their tracks on damp field and woodland tracks, for example, and frequently in snow.

Their powerful legs typically have sturdy feet made for walking or running. The three forward-pointing toes are powerful and have strong, blunt claws suitable for scraping in the soil for food. The claws usually leave clear marks. The toes are widely splayed with a 90° angle between the outer toes. The rear toe is fairly short and somewhat turned in; only the claw leaves a mark.

On the ground, gamebirds move by walking or running, their prints forming a zigzag or an almost straight line.

Pheasant

The pheasant has rather slender toes for a gamebird. Its print is generally fairly pronounced, 6-8 cm long with clear claw marks – including the turned-in rear toe claw. It lives primarily in open woodland and on arable land, where its tracks can be seen alongside fences and on tracks and paths made soggy by rain. It often follows the same route and creates tracks that are best observed on snow, when you will often be able to see marks made by its long tail.

Grey partridge and red-legged partridge

Grey partridge and red-legged partridge prints resemble those of pheasant, but are smaller, only 4-5 cm long. They keep to open ground and prefer fairly dry areas, which in summer means little chance of track prints. In winter, when they travel in small family groups, the tracks are very con-

Pheasant tracks – a characteristic gamebird footprint.

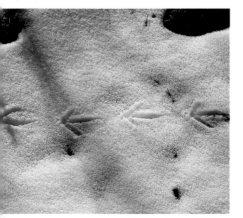

Partridge tracks in firm snow-cover. The birds moved from the foreground of the picture into the background.

In deep, soft snow the partridge's body also leaves a track.

spicuous and appear as winding, often parallel, continuous lines in the snow. The individual footprints are almost always in a
straight line.

Quail

The quail, which is only half the size of the
grey partridge, leaves a print that is 2-2.5
cm long.

Capercaillie track.

Capercaillie

The capercaillie's track is easy to recognise,
purely on the basis of its size. The cock's
print is 10-11 cm long and 8-9 cm wide;
the hen's is smaller. It lives in established
coniferous woodland, where its walking
track creates winding lines among the trees
on the snow-covered forest floor in winter.
At mating sites you can see how the cocks
trail their wings during courtship, making
furrows in the snow along the line of footprints.

Black grouse

Black grouse prints resemble those of capercaillie, but are smaller, 7-8 cm long and 6-7
cm wide. It prefers more open ground than
capercaillie, and its tracks can be found particularly along forest edges, on moors,
heaths and similar places. At mating sites, as
with capercaillies, you can see how the cocks
trail their wings during courtship, leaving
furrows in the snow (see page 248).

Winding ptarmigan tracks up a slope with scattered trees.

Hazel grouse

Hazel grouse prints resemble those of capercaillie and black grouse in shape, but are smaller, 5-5.5 cm long and 4.5-5 cm wide. It lives in hilly country with mixed woodland and scrub, particularly where there are damp hollows with birch and aspen.

Willow grouse, red grouse and ptarmigan

Grouse have feather-clad toes, which cause the track prints, especially in snow, to be vague and blurred and the toe prints to appear very broad. The length of the print is 4-5 cm. Tracks are seen most often on moorland with small bushes, and the lines of prints wind around and between them.

Black grouse track.

Waterbirds

Birds that can swim usually have distinctive webbing that increases the surface area of the foot. This is important for propulsion when swimming. The toes are kept spread, making the sole large, when the foot pushes backward through the water. When the foot is brought forward the toes are kept close together, for minimum resistance. The webbing, which is a fold of thin, tough skin, varies in shape among the groups of web-footed birds and is therefore an important characteristic for track identification.

Tracks from web-footed birds are naturally seen primarily along shorelines, streams and on beaches, but tracks from some of the species can also be found far from water. It is well known that large flocks of black-headed and common gulls follow ploughs in order to eat the exposed insect larvae and worms. In most cases, however, track in such spots will be fairly indistinct and difficult to identify. For a clear foot print, where the webbing can also be seen, a very soft surface is generally necessary, e.g. mud, wet sand or snow.

Swans

Swan prints can be easily recognised by their size. The middle toe of the *mute swan* is approx. 16 cm, the *whooper swan* approx. 14.5 cm and the *Bewick's swan* approx. 11.5 cm long. The webbing connecting the three forward-pointing toes extends with an almost straight front edge right out to the blunt claws. The outer toes are somewhat curved, and the rear toe is short and turned in; only the claw leaves a mark. Due to the heavy weight of the bird the webbing and claws are generally clearly visible in the footprint.

On land swans move by walking, with turned-in feet and a stride length of 30-40 cm.

Geese

Goose prints have the same shape and appearance as those of swans, but can be distinguished from these by their smaller size. In the *greylag goose*, one of the largest geese, the middle toe is around 8.5-9 cm long, in the *bean goose* it is somewhat smaller, roughly 8-9 cm, while in the small *brent goose* it is only 5-5.5 cm long. Geese have strong, broad toes, and as they are large birds that tread heavily, imprints from claws, webbing and toes are often distinct. Since ducks' toes are thinner than those of geese, the width of the toe print is a good distinguishing mark. In addition to beaches and shorelines, goose tracks can also be seen on soft ground in fields where they have been feeding.

Mallard tracks in wet sand.

Ducks

Ducks' feet and their prints largely resemble those of swans and geese, but are smaller and thinner (see goose section above), and their claws are more pointed. The middle toe of a *mallard*, for example, is approx. 5 cm long. The webbing, which has an almost straight front edge, extends right out to the claws, and the outer toes are slightly curved. The rear toe, which is short, has a small web flap in diving ducks, which in very clear tracks leaves a narrow, oblong mark. In surface-feeding ducks the rear toe print is shorter and rounder. It is impossible to distinguish between the tracks of the many duck species.

On land, ducks move with a waddling gait with turned-in toes. The mallard has a stride length of around 15 cm.

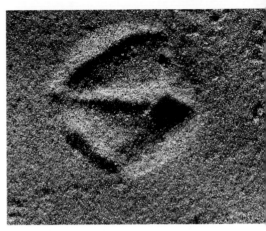

Herring gull footprint.

Gulls

Gulls have webbing between their three forward-pointing toes; it extends right down to the claws and has an almost straight or slightly concave front edge. The outer toes are almost equal. The rear toe is small and so high up that it only leaves marks on very soft ground. The claws are pointed. The length of the *black-headed gull's* middle toe is approx. 3 cm, *common gull's* 3.5 cm, *lesser black-backed gull's* 4.5-5 cm, *herring gull's* 5-5.5 cm, *great black-backed gull's* 6 cm.

Gull tracks are mainly found on the coast, although those of black-headed and common gulls can also frequently be seen far inland. The pointed claws will generally leave marks in the track, but the webbing will only be visible on soft ground. Gulls mainly walk, and occasionally run.

Terns

Unlike gulls, terns' webbing does not extend right out to the claws, and the front edge curves fairly markedly inward. The rear toe is small and the claws pointed. The prints are small; the length of the middle toe for most species is between 2 and 3 cm. Apart from black terns, which frequent marshes and lakes, terns are usually only found on the coast.

Coot

Coots' feet, which leave a very distinctive track, are a cross between a webbed foot and a wading foot. They are very large with long front toes that have large, broad webbing along the side with a deep notch by each toe joint. The middle toe is 8-9.5cm long. The rear toe, which has fairly wide webbing, is just over 3 cm long. Tracks can be observed by lakes and marshes and on beaches.

Waders, herons, storks and cranes

When walking along shallow sandy beaches or the banks of streams or rivers, countless small and medium-sized wader tracks can usually be seen on the sand and mud banks. Due to the huge range of possibilities it is almost impossible to identify the species.

Waders

The characteristic feature of the many species of bird commonly grouped under the term 'waders' is their wading feet. A wading foot has a long, bare midfoot and long, slender front toes with small claws. The rear toe is generally small, and in some species, such as sanderling, may be missing completely. The toes are so widely splayed that the angle between the outer toes is almost 180°. Many waders have incomplete webbing at the base of the toes, but this can rarely be discerned in the track.

Herons and storks

Heron tracks differ somewhat from large wader tracks. In addition to having long, slender front toes, they have a long rear toe, and a large pointed claw on each toe. The long rear toe is undoubtedly connected with the fact that herons spend a lot of time in trees and need to be able to grip branches. Their prints are easy to recognise by their size, the long rear toe and the distinct claw marks. The grey heron's middle toe is 7-8 cm long. Tracks can be seen along lakeshores and coastal inlets.

Mudflats with multiple bird tracks – redshank and other waders have been at work here. Note the round holes from their beaks along the tracks.

Heron tracks in snow along a river, followed by tracks of a carnivore (probably a fox).

Stork tracks can be distinguished from those of herons by their somewhat shorter and much broader toe prints and the small rear toe, that is high up and leaves only a round mark.

Cranes

Crane prints are the same size as grey herons', but with a distinct difference: the rear toe is small and usually leaves no mark. At breeding time tracks can be seen on vegetation-free spots in swamps and marshes, but can otherwise be found along riverbanks and in fields.

Passerines and pigeons

Passerines, which mainly live in trees and bushes, have a foot suitable for gripping branches: they have long, pointed claws and a relatively long rear toe that can flex forward towards the front toes. They often hunt for food on the ground, but their tracks are rarely seen in summer; in winter, however, they are very common on snow. As they are mostly small, lightweight birds, their tracks are not usually especially clear, but in a thin layer of melting snow you can see fine prints, showing the characteristic features:

Crane footprints.

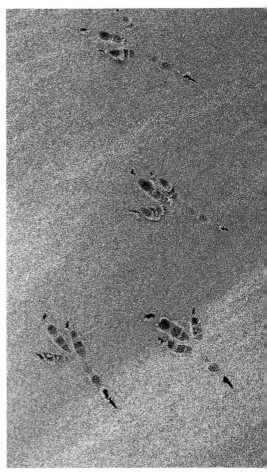

Footprints of wagtail (left) and blackbird (right).

Crow footprints in sand, clearly showing imprints from the ridges under their feet.

long, generally delicate front toes, with an acute angle between the outer toes, a large rear toe and marks made by the long claws.

The *smallest* passerines – e.g. tits and sparrows – usually move by hopping, so their tracks appear in pairs, while the *medium-sized* species – e.g. thrushes – and *large* pas-

serines – e.g. crows – walk and hop. Due to the uneven underside of their feet, crow prints have a distinctive segmented appearance.

Pigeons have feet with large rear toes, like passerines. Tracks are found in fields and woodland and are also common in towns.

95

Pigeon prints in mud.

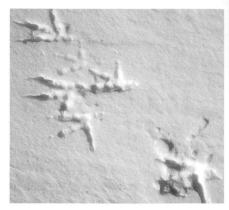

Owl prints in snow. The outer toe is turned out to the side (downward/upward here); the rear toe is small.

The *wood pigeon's* middle toe is approx. 3 cm long. It moves by walking, with turned-in toes and has a stride length of 7-8 cm.

Birds of prey and owls

Buzzard hunting for worms

The feet of birds of prey are adapted in various ways for catching their live food. In those that strike their prey on the ground the toes and claws are mainly short and powerful, while those that catch prey in the air have thinner, longer toes and claws. The osprey's outer toe can turn to the rear (versatile toe) and work together with the rear toe to grip a slippery fish.

Apart from spotted eagles, which walk around on the ground after their prey, and buzzards, which, especially in winter, can be seen waddling around in fields looking for worms and larvae, birds of prey generally stay off the ground, so you rarely find any tracks.

Owls also have well-developed toes and claws. Their foot is special because both the inner and outer toe can function as a versatile toe and work together with the rear toe.

FEEDING
SIGNS

Examples of cones fed on by animals

1. Ripe spruce cone fed on by a squirrel. Ends in a frayed base. The cone will have a somewhat ragged appearance, depending how close to the axis the scales have been gnawed off. Cones such as Sitka spruce and Douglas fir are gnawed in a similar way. Squirrel-gnawed cones are always found on the ground.

2. Seed-scale chewed off by a squirrel. The scale is bitten off whole.

3. Unripe spruce cone fed on by a squirrel.

4. Spruce cone fed on by a mouse. The basal end is evenly rounded with no tip. The close gnawing-off of the scales gives the axis a smooth surface. Mice always feed on loose cones at concealed feeding sites.

5. Spruce cone fed on by a crossbill. The seed-scales have been split longitudinally. Found under the trees.

6. Spruce cone fed on by a woodpecker. Jagged, ruffled appearance. Found at woodpecker anvils, wedged in a crack or lying in large piles below.

7. Ripe pine cone fed on by a squirrel. The cone will be somewhat frayed, depending how closely the scales have been gnawed off. Closely gnawed cones can be confused with mouse-gnawed ones, but squirrel cones are always found on open ground.

8. Unripe pine cone fed on by a squirrel. As the cone is soft and the scales are torn off so it breaks up.

9. Pine cone fed on by a mouse. Scales neatly gnawed off. Found at concealed feeding sites.

10. Pine cone fed on by a wood mouse, while still on the tree, hence the one-sided gnawing.

11. Pine cone fed on by crossbill. Scales forced out from the axis. Found under the trees.

12. Pine cone fed on by a woodpecker. Scales broken lengthways. Found at woodpecker anvils, see no. 6.

13. Cone from Arolla pine fed on by a squirrel. Scales gnawed off uniformly.

14. Larch cone fed on by a squirrel. May vary somewhat, depending whether the scales have been torn off or gnawed off. Found under the trees.

15. Larch cone fed on by a mouse. Feeding site will be hidden.

16. Left, gnawed larch seed with wing. Right, gnawed-off seed-scales.

17. Silver fir cone fed on by a squirrel. Scales torn off.

18. Yew seed fed on by a hawfinch. The seed is split lengthways. Found on the ground under the tree.

19. Yew seed fed on by a marsh tit. The seed is emptied through a fairly regular pecked hole. Found under the feeding site.

20. Yew seed fed on by a nuthatch. Found in bark cracks.

NORWAY
SPRUCE

1 2 3
Squirrel p. 131

4
Mouse p. 132

5
Crossbill p. 135

6
Woodpecker p. 134

7 8
Squirrel p. 131

9 10
Mouse p. 132

11
Crossbill p. 135

12
Woodpecker p. 134

AROLLA PINE

LARCH

SILVER FIR

YEW

Hawfinch
p. 137

18

Marsh
titmouse
p.137

19

Nuthatch
p. 137

20

Squirrel
p. 131

13

14

Squirrel
p. 131

15

16 Mouse
p. 132

Squirrel 17
p. 131

HAZELNUTS
Cultivated varieties
actual size

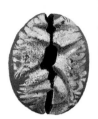

Adult squirrel p. 138   Squirrel-gnawed unripe cluster p. 138   Young squirrel p. 138

Wood mouse p. 141   Bank vole p. 141   Water vole p. 141   Woodpecker p. 142   Woodpecker p. 142
                                                                peck marks   finished

Great tit p. 144   Nuthatch p. 143   Nutcracker p. 144   Magpie p. 144

WALNUTS
actual size

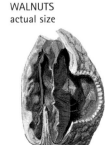
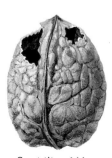
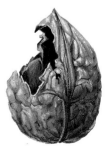

Wood mouse p. 144   Great tit p. 144   Jackdaw p. 144   Crossbill p. 145

BEECHNUT × 1½

Wood mouse p. 145

ACORN × 1½

Wood mouse
p. 146

HORSE CHESTNUT × 1

Wood mouse p. 146

SLOE × 1½

Wood mouse p. 146

ROSEHIP × 2

Squirrel p. 148

CHERRY × 1½

Wood mouse p. 146

Hawfinch p. 147

HAWTHORN × 1½

Bank vole p. 146

Wood mouse p. 148

OATS × 2

Bank vole p. 146

LIME × 1½

Hawfinch p. 146

House mouse p. 150

CHERRY PLUM × 1½

Wood mouse p. 146

HORNBEAM × 1½

Wood mouse p. 146

Rat p. 150

MAIZE × 1½

Wood mouse p. 146

ALMOND × 1½

Greenfinch p. 148

House mouse p. 150

House mouse p. 150

Elk often browse young trees.

If you follow an animal track in the countryside, sooner or later you will come across places where the animal has stopped to eat. These feeding sites may be very close together, as is seen with typical herbivores. For instance, if following a roe deer track, you will see that one moment it stops to graze a little and shortly after stops again to nibble some small twigs from a tree. However, if it is a predator's track, for example a fox, you may cover large distances before observing that the animal has succeeded in killing any prey. In snow you can see where the fox has stopped, often in vain, to investigate a tussock or stump in the hope of surprising a mouse or finding something else edible.

The number of feeding sites is naturally connected with the individual species' choice of food and eating habits. If the food is very nutrient-rich, the animal only needs to eat a relatively small amount to fulfil its requirements, and you will find only a few feeding sites. However, if the food is poor in nutritional value, the animal must eat a lot and often, and the number of feeding sites increases. Typical examples are the wood mouse and the field vole. A large part of the wood mouse's diet consists of seed, which is very nutrient-rich, and it can therefore manage by eating relatively little. This also means that it need only be active at night, which for safety reasons is the best time. The field vole, however, feeds chiefly on grass, which is so poor in nutrients that it has to fill its stomach several times a day. Therefore this species has to be active both day and night in order to survive.

Most animals prefer to remain more or less hidden when eating. So small rodents will generally take their food to a special feeding site under a tussock, a pile of twigs or a similar spot, where they can be in relative safety while busy eating.

However, some animal's feeding sites are out in the open and are very conspicuous. This includes large predators, which generally have nothing to be afraid of, and animals like birds of prey and squirrels, which typically orient themselves by sight and are therefore capable of spotting any enemies approaching in good time.

Some feeding sites, e.g. those where deer have peeled off bark or where bank voles have gnawed bark, are very conspicuous and can be identified even after several years.

However, animals' feeding sites are usually erased relatively quickly. This is particularly true of predator's feeding sites, and you should be aware, with these in particular, that several different species may have used the same feeding site.

It is common for smaller carnivores to take advantage of remains from larger carnivores' meals.

A closer investigation of an animal's

Silver fir, with its top branches bitten off by a hare – for no obvious reason.

At some feeding sites it is easier to identify species than at others. This is one of the more difficult: a water vole has been feeding on fat-hen.

feeding site will always provide a lot of interesting information on the animal in question. It can not only tell you about the animal's choice of food and the way it eats, but, based on its location and appearance, it is often possible to read much more about the animal's behaviour.

Remains or leftovers from animals' meals may show signs of handling by the species in question, and you will nearly always be able to find marks on them from the animal's teeth or beak. The marks themselves are generally called 'feeding signs', and for remains at a predator's feeding site in particular the term 'prey' is often used.

On the basis of all the observations regarding choice of food, feeding signs, method of handling the food etc. that can

be made at a feeding site, you will nearly always be able to determine what type of animal has used that particular feeding site. With a little practice it may even be possible to identify the species.

As an aid to this fascinating and absorbing detective work, the following section provides a description of the most common feeding sites, divided up according to where they occur: on trees and bushes, fruits, herbs etc. Under each individual type of feeding site, feeding signs are discussed in more detail, divided up according to animal group. There are further subdivisions according to the part of the food material the marks appear on; e.g. gnawing on bark or roots, or predators' marks on birds or mammals.

Feeding signs on trees and bushes

Bark, twigs and buds, especially from young trees and bushes, play a huge role as food for many animals in winter. This includes species of deer and goat, hares, numerous small rodents and squirrels. In most cases the marks from the animal's teeth will stand out fairly distinctly in the bark, and the size and appearance of the individual tooth-marks are excellent clues for identifying the type of animal.

Feeding signs left by birds, which you can see particularly on mature trees, are of a more indirect nature, e.g. pecking marks in bark caused by insect-eating birds, especially woodpeckers, in their search for food.

It is usually easy to determine whether a feeding trace comes from an animal with teeth or was made by a bird. Toothmarks appear either as crescent-shaped marks, two or more side by side, or as deep parallel grooves, resembling marks from a gouge. Beak marks appear as distinct notches.

A straight 'tide-line' on isolated trees is a sign of browsing by deer.

Heights reached by various animals when gnawing bark. Snow-cover allows them to reach higher up in winter.

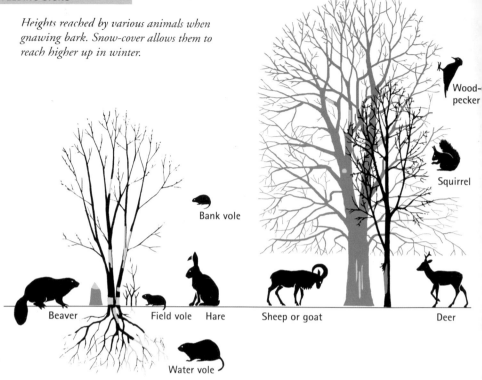

Wood-pecker

Squirrel

Bank vole

Beaver   Field vole   Hare   Sheep or goat   Deer

Water vole

Roe deer skull. Like other deer, it has no upper incisors. This has a major influence on how deer obtain food.

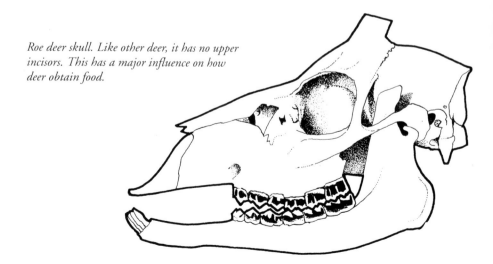

Two examples of deer gnawing on spruce trunks. The trunk on the left has been gnawed by an elk, while that on the right has been exposed to red deer gnawing, which is almost as intense.

Deer

In addition to the size and appearance of the marks, their position on the tree can be significant in identification (see diagram).

With regard to deer 'attacks' on tree bark, you should be aware of the difference between barking (see page 109) and fraying (see page 241). In barking, the animal eats the bark, leaving toothmarks, while fraying leaves scratches in bark and wood caused by the antlers.

In winter the various species of deer feed partly on bark, buds and shoot tips from trees and bushes – both deciduous and evergreen. Feeding signs of bitten-off twigs and branches are described simply as 'bites', while the term 'peeling' is used when it involves bark.

Given the size of deer it is not surprising that their feeding signs are very conspicuous and often of an intense nature. To interpret and completely understand the appearance of these feeding marks, however, it is necessary to know a bit about the animals' teeth.

In deer, which are ruminants, the upper incisors have been replaced by a keratinised plate, which the lower incisors bite up against. This distinctive mouth structure means that when a deer nibbles shoot tips and small twigs the effect is more like breaking or tearing off rather than normal biting. The fracture is therefore uneven and ragged – not smooth, as would be the case if bitten off by a hare (see page 112). With slightly

The basal growth on this spruce is a result of nibbling by deer.

Different ways of biting off shoot tips result in widely differing appearances.

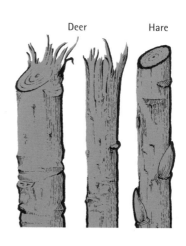

Deer   Hare

thicker twigs in particular you can often clearly see that one edge of the fracture is uneven and ragged. When deer use their molars for biting, the bite rim is always totally ragged.

Browsing

The leading shoots of small trees are especially susceptible to being nibbled by deer, and it is obviously serious for trees to lose these particular shoots, as it prevents them from growing properly. Young trees, which for one reason or another are in particular danger and therefore continually having their outer shoot tips bitten off, gradually assume a dense conical shape like a well-clipped hedge. If one of these trees manages to send out a shoot so high up that the deer can no longer reach the top, this will develop normally, producing one of the delightful trees with a dense 'foot muff' of small branches round the bottom.

In areas with large deer populations, they will also leave their mark on large trees. This is especially clear in deer parks, where crowns of isolated trees and trees along woodland fringes have been sharply clipped in a characteristic way at the bottom at a fairly specific height – the height to which the deer have been able to reach. Bitten-off forest fringes and 'foot muffs' can also be seen, caused by their browsing.

Barking

The eating of bark by deer – or barking as it is also called – occurs in two forms, summer barking and winter barking. These names have no direct relation to the seasons, as you might expect, but refer rather to the condition of the bark.

When the sap is rising in the trees, i.e. when they are growing, the bark is 'loose', and the animal's eating results in *summer barking*. Most summer barking therefore takes place early in spring. When the bark is loose, the animal presses its incisors into the bark at the bottom of the trunk, grasps the freed edge firmly with its teeth and pulls, tearing the bark off in long strips and exposing the wood.

In winter, when the bark adheres firmly to the wood, you have *winter barking*. This

Cross-section of 40-year-old Norway spruce. After about 10 years (shaded area) the tree was subjected to red deer barking for the first time, affecting more than 2/3 of the trunk's circumference. Since then the tree has been subjected to barking at regular intervals, each time resulting in rot and growing over. A trunk like this may be an interesting shape, but is worthless as timber.

Two examples of trunks barked by fallow deer. Left, cypress and right, elm.

is almost like a planing of the bark, and the marks from the lower incisors can be seen as clear furrows on the trunk surface, as the innermost layer of bark remains as narrow bands between the marks from the individual teeth.

Barking normally only occurs on one side of a tree, so it does not die, but can overcome the damage and close the wound by growing over. However, barking retards the growth of a tree, and the bare wood is often attacked by various saprophytic fungi. Growing over also makes the bottom and most valuable section of the trunk worthless as timber.

Feeding signs of individual deer species

Although there are of course differences in the width of the toothmarks, and the height to which the various species can reach to nibble and bark, feeding signs on trees and bushes are mostly similar. However, the frequency with which the various species feed on woody plants varies somewhat, and there are also variations within the individual species from place to place.

Elk: In winter elk feed almost exclusively on shoot tips, leaves and bark from various trees and bushes. Due to their huge size their feeding signs are massive, including se vered branches, and they may sometimes knock trees over by walking in over the trunk and pushing it down so that it breaks, in order to get at high twigs.

Red deer, fallow deer and sika deer: These species nibble and bark, but not as violently as elk, and it can be difficult to distinguish between the feeding marks of the three species.

Roe deer: Roe deer feed largely on buds and shoot tips of various woody plants in winter, but barking occurs occasionally.

Reindeer: In summer reindeer eat leaves and shoots from various bushes, but bark is not part of their diet.

Muntjac: The muntjac comes from Asia and has been introduced into England and France. It nibbles twigs and, to a small degree, peels bark from branches and small trees.

White-tailed deer: This deer has been introduced into Finland from America. It nibbles twigs and peels bark.

Sheep and goats

Sheep and *goats,* like deer, are ruminants. Their upper incisors have been replaced by a hardened plate (see also p. 106). Like deer, they often eat twigs and bark, and their feeding signs can be confused with those of deer. However, when peeling bark, the marks from their lower incisors will generally be at an oblique angle in relation to the length of the tree, while the toothmarks of deer mainly go along the trunk.

Where sheep and goats are kept as livestock it is particularly common in winter to see them barking trees. The same happens

Young oaks barked by mouflon. Note that they have all been barked at the same height.

in woodland in areas where, as in Denmark for example, *mouflon* have been introduced as game. The mouflon is a wild sheep that comes from Corsica and Sardinia.

Rodents, rabbits and hares

Rodents, rabbits and hares feed predominantly on vegetable food, which in winter they partially obtain by gnawing trees and bushes. Their feeding signs are commonly described as 'gnawing'.

To interpret the marks they leave at feeding sites you need to know a bit about the 'tools' and technique they use when gnawing. The 'tools' are the large, curved front teeth, the *incisors*, of which there are two

upper and two lower. Members of the hare family have four upper incisors (immediately behind the large incisors are another pair that do not leave marks when gnawing).

The incisors are positioned a long way forward in the mouth, separated from the

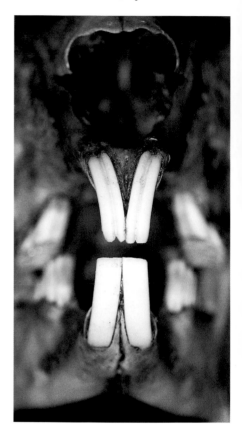

A hare's incisors. The upper jaw has an extra set of incisors behind those you can see. This is the case for all members of the rabbit family, but rodents only have one set of upper incisors. Note that the upper incisors have a longitudinal groove in the centre.

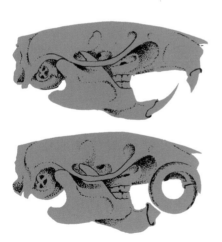

Top, rat skull, showing the sharp incisors used for gnawing etc. Below shows abnormal continuous growth of the teeth when not counteracted by wear, so they have become far to long.

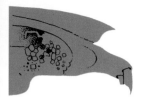 

Hare's upper jaw seen in cross section (left) and from below (right). Behind the large incisors a smaller set is visible. Compare the photograph on the previous page.

molars by a large, toothless gap. They grow continually so that they can keep pace with the substantial wear caused by the gnawing. Rats' teeth grow 2.7 mm per week and wear at an equivalent rate. If an incisor grows crooked for one reason or another, so that it does not wear correctly, it will continue to grow unimpeded and eventually make it difficult or impossible for the animal to eat, until it may finally starve to death.

The front and part of the side surfaces of the incisors are coated with enamel, while the back either lacks enamel or has only a fairly thin layer, like the hare's. This uneven distribution of the hard enamel means that the tooth wears obliquely, creating a sharp incisal edge, which is constantly sharpened by gnawing.

Most rodents have a cleft in their upper lip, a 'harelip', so the incisors can work freely and unconstrained, and by the gap between the incisors and the molars on the inside of the lips are some pads that can close off the rear section of the oral cavity, preventing the animal getting chippings in its mouth when gnawing.

The actual gnawing is done principally by the lower incisors, while the upper incisors are used to keep the head stationary while gnawing. The upper incisors therefore generally only leave fairly short, often slightly curved marks, while the lower ones leave long grooves. It is important to be clear about this, as you often have to use the shape and appearance of the toothmarks to identify what animal has left a certain set of marks.

There are three types of gnawing: root-gnawing, bark-gnawing and bud-gnawing.

Root-gnawing

Water vole: During the summer water voles feed on above-ground parts of plants. In autumn they collect a winter cache of juicy stemwood, swollen roots, bulbs, seeds etc., which is stored in large stockpiles connected to their underground tunnel system. During the winter they live mainly underground, feeding on the collected cache and roots of trees and bushes.

Gnawing on roots is very intense, and the entire central section of the root system is often gnawed away, so the tree becomes quite unsteady and is easily knocked down.

As the water vole is a large animal – rat sized – its gnawing is vigorous and the toothmarks large and distinct. The overall width of the mark from two upper incisors is 3.5-4 mm.

Unlike field voles, water voles rarely attack very young trees, but, on the other hand, can completely gnaw roots off trees with a trunk diameter of 20-30 cm.

Water voles prefer deciduous trees, but gnaw conifers too, and would probably attack any woody species. In continental Europe they sometimes damage apple trees.

113

As mentioned, winter gnawing normally takes place hidden underground, but sometimes root-gnawing may continue as bark-gnawing above ground on the bottom sections of the trunk. This occurs where trees are surrounded by tall, dense grassy vegetation, and only takes place at the end of winter or very early in spring.

Primarily because of its activities as a root-gnawer, the water vole can be a pest, and in some areas causes major annual losses for fruit growers, nurseries and forestry. In Britain, however, they are rather local, and tend to be found in clear rivers and streams.

Field vole: Field voles, which are especially noted for their above-ground bark-gnawing (see page 116), also often forage on underground parts of woody plants in winter. They may gnaw through young tree roots just under the surface, especially small beech trees and oaks up to 2-3 cm thick. The vole simply gnaws away a section of the root, which often causes the young tree to over-balance and topple over. If you dig down, you will find that, apart from the gnawing-through, the root is in fairly good condition (compare water vole above).

The gnawed-away section will generally be 5-10 cm long. It is often not completely gnawed through, and the two sections of root are connected by a sliver consisting of a strip of bark and a little wood.

Water vole winter gnawing on the root of an apple tree. It eats not just the bark but the whole root, so the tree topples easily in stormy weather.

The gnawed surfaces can be straight across, but are often sloping, due to the vole gnawing from the side and into the root. The toothmarks can be seen very clearly on the actual gnawing surface, and from their small size it is easy to distinguish this from the water vole's very vigorous gnawing. The overall width of the mark from the two upper incisors is approx. 2.5 mm.

Bark-gnawing

Bark plays an important role for many rodents and for hares and wild rabbits, but they usually only use bark, which is poor in nutritional value, to get them through adverse and lean periods. The beaver is an ex-

Root sections gnawed by field vole.

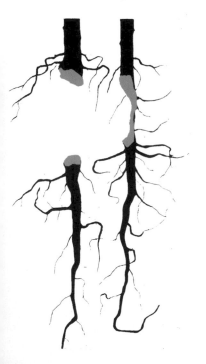

A field vole has gnawed off the bark all the way round this rowan. Marks from the incisors are clearly visible.

ception; bark is its most important food all year round.

Therefore most bark-gnawing takes place in winter, although you may also observe bark-gnawing in summer by field voles, bank voles, water voles and squirrels, as well as beavers.

In most cases you will be able to see the individual toothmarks in the bark. Looking at these and the manner of gnawing and its position on the tree should generally allow relatively easy identification of the animal responsible.

115

In addition, bark-gnawing is very conspicuous, and compared with most other feeding signs very long-lasting, and can often be identified after several months, sometimes even years.

Field vole: Field voles are found in areas with dense grassy ground cover. In winter you are almost certain to see their bark-gnawing on young trees that have dense grass between them. Their attacks are often so extensive that they have been described as 'woodland's enemy no. 1'. They also have a major financial impact on orchards.

In captivity field voles have been shown to be quite capable of climbing trees, but in the wild it is extremely rare. When gnawing bark, the vole normally sticks to the sections it can reach from the ground – generally the bottom 10-15 cm. The gnawing is therefore very concentrated and deep, and the trees are often gnawed all the way round and subsequently die.

If there are twigs or similar for the vole to sit on, the gnawing will extend further upwards than the aforementioned 10-15 cm; snow-cover will also help it reach higher than normal.

The bark is often gnawed off right down to the wood, and the toothmarks can be clearly seen on its surface. Marks from the upper incisors are best seen on the edges of the remaining bark, where they leave two faintly crescent-shaped markings with an overall width of around 2.5mm. The two pointed lower incisors leave thin grooves that are clearly visible on the surface of the wood.

Field voles prefer deciduous bark, but conifers – particularly soft-barked species – are also often attacked, and by and large any

species could be gnawed. They can cause damage to apple trees in orchards.

Bark-gnawing by field voles normally occurs in winter, but they sometimes also gnaw bark in July-August. This summer gnawing differs in several ways from winter gnawing. In winter the vole eats most of the gnawed-off bark, but in summer it does not eat any. The bark, which is very loose at this time of year due to the tree's growth, is bitten off in small pieces, which can be found at the foot of the trunk. When the bark is bitten off, part of the cambium remains on the trunk, and this is the layer the vole is seeking. On the bare surfaces you can see how it has scraped off the cambium very carefully with its incisors. The numerous fine toothmarks make the bare wood surface fairly rough.

A special type of bark-gnawing, *stick-gnawing*, can be observed on or in the immediate vicinity of field vole tracks. Here you will sometimes find little groups of small, peeled sticks, varying in length from a few cm up to around 20 cm, and up to almost 1cm thick. The ends bear clear marks of having been gnawed, and along the sides are numerous delicate toothmarks.

These sticks most resemble miniature 'beaver-sticks' (see page 122) and are produced by the field vole in an identical fashion. To get at the bark, the non-climbing field vole fells a shoot by gnawing around the bottom in the same way that a beaver deals with a sapling. It then gnaws off a suitable piece and hauls it off to a special feeding spot, where the actual debarking takes place, and where the finished sticks gradually accumulate. Stick-gnawing can often be observed in raspberry and black-

Stick-gnawing by field vole. Left, raspberry shoots, right, small conifer twigs, seen completely debarked on top of some spruce needles.

berry stands, and is also common where snow has weighed down young conifer branches, allowing the voles to reach and bite off twigs. In this instance you will find all the needles, which the animals do not eat, at the feeding site, along with the debarked sticks.

Bank vole: Like field voles, bank voles are very active bark-gnawers, but they are also very capable climbers, so signs of their activities should be looked for up in the trees.

In spring it is very common to see elders in woodland with large sections of the trunk and the larger branches completely debarked, with the gleaming white wood visible from afar. This is the work of the bank vole in winter. Trees up to 20-30 cm thick are attacked, and the gnawing can extend several metres up into the tree.

On the ground under gnawed trees you will often find – particularly in towards the trunk – a thick layer of small, bitten-off bark fragments. This is the thick outer layer

117

Bank vole gnawing on bark high up in a Douglas fir.

from the bank vole's two upper incisors have an overall width of 1.5-2 mm.

As bank vole bark-gnawing generally occurs scattered up in the trees, it is normally not nearly so devastating as damage caused by field voles. Bank vole gnawing occurs mostly in winter during the lean period, but, like field voles, they may also gnaw bark in July-August, and this does not appear to be due to normal hunger.

Summer gnawing, which largely resembles that of field voles (see page 116) but occurs up in the trees, is deeper and more destructive than winter gnawing.

The distinctive *stick-gnawing*, familiar among field voles (see page 117), also occurs with bank voles, and it is difficult to distinguish between the two. Sticks gnawed by bank voles can be found under fresh heaps of brushwood.

Water vole: Water voles, which are known for their root gnawing, may also gnaw bark in summer. The gnawing, which is very distinctive, is similar to field and bank vole summer gnawing, but is only found on ash.

As water voles cannot climb, they can only gnaw the ash trunks as high as they can reach from the ground, i.e. approx. 20 cm, usually resulting in complete ringgnawing of the trees. The bark, which water voles do not eat but leave on the ground, is bitten off in very distinctive 0.5-1 cm-wide strips, usually with a marked curve at one end. Toothmarks are clearly visible along the edges of the bark strips and the remaining bark.

The distinctive shape is caused by the animal finishing the strips by gnawing along the trunk, while the rest of the time it gnaws across.

of bark, consisting of cork; the vole is not interested in this and therefore discards it. However, the inner, living section of the bark is readily eaten.

Bank voles attack conifers as well as deciduous trees, favouring the more soft-barked varieties. The gnawing usually begins in the angle of the branch, where the voles can sit comfortably while gnawing. From here it spreads up the trunk, and out along the branches, and in the worst cases trees may be completely debarked from top to bottom.

Gnawing by bank voles is usually not as deep and vigorous as that of field voles, as they are smaller and weaker animals. The wood of the gnawed surfaces is therefore often more or less covered with bark remnants, forming a thin, brown layer, finely furrowed by vole teeth. The toothmarks

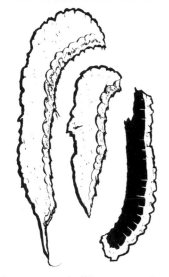

Bark strips gnawed off by a water vole.

Water vole summer gnawing on an ash, show-ing marks from the teeth on the surface of the wood. On the ground at the foot of the tree are the bitten-off bark strips.

After gnawing away the bark the water vole rasps off and eats the layer of cambium left on the trunk, leaving the surface of the wood with a distinctive, rough appearance, and countless toothmarks.

Water vole attacks on ash trees character-istically only last a fairly short time. How-ever they work so fast that they can destroy several hundred trees in just a few days.

Beaver: The beaver, Europe's largest rodent, has some extremely distinctive feeding signs that cannot be confused with any other animal's.

Its diet consists primarily of bark, twigs and leaves, and as it has to eat a lot due to its size and the food's relatively poor nutri-tional value, its feeding sites are large and very conspicuous.

It favours gnawing deciduous trees – es-pecially aspen – but also alder, willow and birch. It very seldom removes bark from conifers.

To get at the bark, beavers fell even very large trees, and beaver localities always dis-play highly distinctive characteristics. They gnaw across the trunk on all sides at a height of roughly half a metre. This pro-duces an hourglass-shaped narrowing, which eventually causes the tree to topple over. Slender trees, however, can be felled by gnawing from just one side; and thin branches are bitten directly in two, leaving a clean edge.

A beaver's bite is very powerful, and when felling trees it bites off chips up to 3-4 cm wide and 10-12 cm long. Toothmarks, which are approx. 8 mm wide, are clearly visible on both trees and chips.

In autumn they bite off thinner branches in suitable lengths and transport them to

Wood shaving gnawed off by a beaver. Toothmarks can be seen on the right.

Beaver feeding site.

Partially debarked birch log, with beaver toothmarks clearly visible.

Beavers do not always fell trees to debark them. In this instance some Scots pines have been ringed at the base.

their dwelling, where they are stored as a winter cache. Branches up to 10cm in diameter, sometimes even thicker, are gnawed off in sections approx. 1m long and dragged to the feeding site, located at the water's edge. They are debarked here and then used as building timber in beaver lodges and dams.

The gnawed branch sections, 'beaver sticks', can occasionally be found preserved under peat, sometimes in places from which beavers disappeared thousands of years ago. A fascinating relic from the distant past.

Squirrel: Squirrels sometimes gnaw bark, but as this usually – if not always – occurs in the summer period, while the trees are growing and the bark is therefore loose, it is more like barking than actual gnawing: so it is usually referred to as squirrel barking.

The barking occurs up in the trees, and the bark is stripped off in short or long strips, leaving sharp bark edges with no toothmarks.

The bark is not eaten, but is left on the ground under the stripped tree. However, squirrels will rasp off and eat the layer of cambium left on the wood once the bark has been pulled off. The rasping-off of the cambium leaves only very faint toothmarks on the surface of the wood, and it is possible that it is the sap the animal is after, and that it is partially licked off.

Barking can occur on both deciduous and coniferous trees. One distinctive feature is that it is trunk bark only that is attacked, never bark on branches.

On older conifers, the thin bark at the tops of the trees is particularly prone to at-

Squirrel gnawing for bark beetle larvae. The circular holes going into the wood are tunnels in which the larvae pupated.

tack. This debarking often causes the top to die and eventually snap off.

Hare, mountain hare and rabbit: The gnawing of these animals on trees and bushes leaves very distinctive marks, which are easy to distinguish from other animals' feeding signs. However, they resemble one another extremely closely and are difficult to tell apart.

In winter particularly, but also to some extent in summer, hares and rabbits bite off and eat twigs from young trees. So you often see young trees that are especially exposed growing into branching bushes, as the constant biting of the twigs prevents them from growing upwards. Both coniferous and deciduous trees are nibbled.

The bitten-off twigs are often not eaten, and you see them lying untouched around the affected tree, almost as if the nibbling is just for amusement. At *mountain hare* feeding sites in winter you can see the buds from the twigs left in the snow, strange as it may seem, as if the animal has deliberately

Hares also gnaw bark off smaller branches. Note that the gnawing marks go across the branch. The narrow marks from the upper incisors are seen in the centre of the branch and those from the broader lower teeth towards the sides (see also photograph, page 112).

Deep and destructive gnawing on a fruit tree, where snowdrifts have allowed hares to reach high up.

avoided eating them, even though the buds are particularly nutrient-rich. They mainly eat the bark, and whole heaps of brushwood can be found stripped.

The actual bite rims are very distinctive, as the animals' sharp incisors produce a smooth, oblique cut, as if made by a sharp knife. They are thus easy to distinguish from the ragged bites left by deer (see page 109).

In winter, *hares* and *rabbits* often gnaw bark and can cause significant damage in woodland and orchards. Their gnawing is very vigorous and can be easily recognised by the toothmarks. It actually looks as if the gnawing has been done by an animal with four narrow upper teeth and two broad lower teeth. However, this is due to the fact that the two upper incisors each have a deep longitudinal groove that leaves a narrow strip of bark in the toothmarks.

Bud-gnawing

The nutrient-rich buds of woody plants are often eaten in winter by mice, bank voles and squirrels, which can climb well.

Mice and voles: Among small rodents it is *bank voles* in particular, and also *wood mice* and *yellow-necked mice,* that gnaw buds. Gnawing signs left by the various mouse species is so similar that they cannot be distinguished from one another. They gnaw a hole in the side of the bud and scrape out the contents using their long, pointed lower incisors, leaving the bud scales like a hollow case. Complete gnawing-off of the bud may also occur, generally leaving the bottom bud scale behind like a little bowl.

It is often vegetative buds of young trees that are attacked, and repeated bud-gnawing can cause trees to become bushy.

A bank vole has gnawed some of the terminal buds of this silver fir. Repeated bud-gnawing can cause young trees to become bushy.

Bud-gnawing seems particularly to affect conifers, especially silver fir and larch, but is also often seen on deciduous trees. For example, if you examine an elder that has been exposed to bank vole bark-gnawing, you will often see that a large number of the buds have been gnawed off. And there will probably be indications that this happened before the bark-gnawing really began.

Squirrel: In the winter following years with poor seed production, quantities of small, green twigs can often be observed forming a carpet under established stands of Norway spruce. It was formerly believed that the trees themselves were casting off the twigs for one reason or another, and the phenomenon was called 'shedding'. We now know that this is the work of squirrels.

The twigs are generally 5-10 cm long, and you can see by the even break that they have been bitten off. They can be distinguished in this way from twigs torn off in stormy weather, which have a ragged break. If you examine the bitten-off twigs more closely, they are all year-old shoots, bitten off just under the ring of male-flower buds at the base of the shoot. All these buds, which are particularly nutrient-rich, have been scooped out and emptied by squirrels, and only the cup-shaped case of the cover remains. It is amazing that an animal as large as a squirrel can empty a bud without causing more damage to the outer case. Often only the odd bud scale has been torn off. The reason is that it pokes one of its long, pointed lower incisors in at the bottom of the bud and fishes out the core. Sometimes individual vegetative buds fur-

Spruce twigs bitten off by a squirrel, which has eaten the female flower buds.

ther out on the twig are also scooped out, but the terminal bud is generally undamaged.

Squirrels' bud-gnawing is, as mentioned, particularly common on Norway spruce,

Norway spruce twig with male flowers that have been emptied by a squirrel. See also photograph above.

but occurs on sitka spruce, silver fir, larch and other conifers, and can also be seen on beech. For an approx. 60-year-old stand of spruce it is estimated that squirrels in a winter with few cones, but numerous flower buds, would on average bite off 1,200 twigs per tree.

Squirrels' feeding signs can sometimes assume a somewhat different character. You can see that it gnaws the shoot in two a little way up to get to the large, thick buds on a silver fir's top shoot. Sap flow soon obliterates the toothmarks, and the bite rim will be indistinguishable from that of a deer bite. However, the height of the marks will generally rule out the possibility of it being caused by deer. If you remove the sap, you can clearly see that it is caused by gnawing not biting.

Birds

The most obvious bird feeding signs on woody plants are caused by woodpeckers. In their search for insects, larvae and pupae in the bark cracks and crevices they peck with their powerful beak, causing the bark to fray or flake off. The tip of the beak, which is compressed and shaped like a small chisel, leaves long, narrow marks on the trunk. This type of feeding trace is most marked in areas where the three-toed woodpecker is common (mainly north-east Europe and mountains of central Europe). Such signs, on Scots pine for example, may be visible from afar – the outer, dark, crusty bark layer may be completely pecked off, giving the trunk an unnatural colouring.

Black woodpecker.

Diagram of a woodpecker's head, showing its long tongue that can be extended approx. 10 cm out of its beak. It is anchored close to the nostril.

and chips 10-15 cm long and several cm wide can be found on the ground. Although the black woodpecker is the size of a crow, the tremendous power it possesses is nevertheless astonishing. Tree stumps and older

Woodpeckers

Woodpeckers get at larvae and adult insects living inside the wood by pecking holes in the trunk and fishing their prey out using their extremely long, sticky tongue with barbs along the edge. Beak marks are generally clearly visible at the sides of the hole and on the chips lying on the ground.

Feeding signs of this type are most pronounced from *black woodpeckers* pecking for carpenter ants. These large ants, which are much sought-after by black woodpeckers, often live in conifers, and their tunnels may extend several metres up inside the trunk. The tunnels are often deep inside the trunk surrounded by a thick layer of healthy wood, so it is a huge job for the woodpecker to get to the ants. The holes are very large, up to half a metre long and 10-15 cm wide,

Spruce pecked by black woodpecker.

wind-felled trunks can also be found completely hacked to pieces and broken up by black woodpeckers. This woodpecker is expanding its range in continental Europe, but is only a rare vagrant to Britain.

It is common for woodpeckers, particularly *great spotted woodpeckers,* to peck grooves in trunks and thick branches, in which to wedge cones or nuts, while they work on them (see page 134). These woodpecker 'anvils' can always be identified by the food remains, either left in the hole or lying on the ground below.

Woodpeckers sometimes peck short or long grooves – or a series of grooves or holes – around tree trunks. This is most often seen on young trees, and it is believed that the woodpeckers lick up the sap which oozes out.

Other birds

Many other birds eat buds, nibbling them off with their beaks and leaving no particularly distinctive marks. Flower buds are particularly sought after, and finches, notably *bullfinches,* can cause major damage on fruit trees. Woody plants' buds and catkins play an important role in winter for *black grouse, hazel grouse* and *grouse,* and the fresh shoots and needles of Scots pine are the most important food of the capercaillie. Capercaillies often prefer to forage in quite specific trees, which may then be almost completely stripped of needles.

The three-toed woodpecker's distinctive peck marks in the bark of a spruce.

127

Feeding signs on seeds, fruit and herbaceous plants

The fruits, and particularly the seeds, of plants contain a strong concentration of reserves, mainly in the form of oil, starch and proteins. These substances, which are intended for the initial formation of new plants, are much sought-after by various animals due to their high nutritive value. Many rodents and birds survive during the adverse period of the year almost exclusively by eating fruits. The reason squirrels and crossbills, for example, can breed while it is still winter is undoubtedly largely due to the fact that the spruce cones at that exact time are full of ripe seeds, so they have no trouble obtaining high-calorie food for their young.

The vast majority of seeds end up in a pulverised state in an animal's stomach, but nevertheless it is a great biological advantage for plants to have fruit or seeds that are sought after by animals. For example, a woodpecker may lose its spruce cone en route to its 'anvil', the yellow-necked mouse may be caught by an owl before having eaten all its winter cache of beechnuts, or the squirrel may forget where it buried its collection of nuts. All this means that the plants, with the animals' help, have managed to spread their seed to new habitats. This form of seed dispersal is called animal dispersal.

Cones on a silver fir gnawed by a wood mouse.

A smaller percentage of seeds are swallowed whole and pass through the animal unharmed, leaving via the droppings or pellets, possibly some distance from the place where they were eaten. There will be no marks on such seeds to give clues to the animal's species. However, identification can be made from the additional content and the form of the droppings or pellets.

When an animal eats fruit, however, there will generally be some remains left at the feeding site, and in many cases it is possible to identify the animal from the teeth or beak marks on these remains.

As most fruits are taken by some animal or other, the category 'animal-gnawed fruits' is in reality hugely comprehensive. In the following section we mention only a few of the most common cases you may come across in the garden or on outings in the countryside.

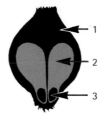

Spruce cone. Right, a cross section of a cone with the seeds shown in black – note that they are on the upperside of the scales. Left, a scale (1) seen from above. The seed (3) lies at the base and has a wing (2), which the wind can catch and carry the seed to a new habitat.

Cones

Conifer seeds are an extremely important food for many rodents and birds, and feeding sites with partly-eaten cones are therefore very common and can be found almost everywhere in established coniferous woodland.

A cone such as that of Norway spruce consists of a central axis with a large number of helicoid, overlapping double scales, the ovuliferous scale and bract scale. The ovuliferous scale, which is largest, is closest to the axis and bears two seeds on the inside. Each seed has a membranous wing. The bract scale is much smaller and is found at the base of the other. In Douglas fir the bract scales are longer than the ovuliferous scales and protrude, with a three-lobed tip.

The seeds mature in autumn, but as long as the weather stays damp, the ovuliferous scales remain tightly closed to protect and retain the seeds. Only in spring, when sun and wind dry the cone out, will the scales open. Pine cones do not mature until at least their second year.

Gradually, as the cones mature, the scales lignify and eventually become so hard that it often takes a huge amount of effort for an animal to get to the seeds. This will leave distinct marks, different from species to species, and it is generally easy to determine what animal has fed on the cone.

Yew cones, often known as berry cones, have a substantially different structure: they consist of a relatively large thick-husked seed surrounded by a juicy aril that is first green and later a beautiful red. Yew needles are known to contain a toxin that livestock, particularly horses, are very sensitive to, but the fruits (aril flesh) are non-poisonous to birds – and much sought-after.

Part of yew twig with 'berries'.

Squirrel feeding site on a tree stump.

Squirrel

Cones are a very important food, especially for red squirrels, and conifer seeds form the bulk of their diet for a large part of the year. As the individual seeds are very small, however, a squirrel must dismantle a large number of cones to fulfil its food requirement.

Squirrels primarily forage up in the trees, and damaged cone axes and gnawed-off scales can be found evenly scattered on the ground underneath. They often have a favourite feeding site, and below it you will find hundreds of partly-eaten cones.

Fallen cones, however, are generally gnawed on the ground. The squirrel will usually sit on a little hillock or tree stump, so it has a good view all around and can spot possible danger in plenty of time. At such feeding sites the gnawed cone axes and scales will be gathered in a little pile. Norway spruce cones fed on by squirrels may vary somewhat in appearance, but one thing common to almost all cones is that the basal end has a short or long tip, sometimes frayed.

Squirrels begin gnawing at the base of the cone, holding it tilted with their forepaws, generally with the top end resting downwards. The scales at the base are fairly small, often without seeds, and so loose that the squirrel can easily tear them off with its teeth. Some of the cone axis is often torn off at the same time, producing the characteristic frayed tip (see page 99).

When it cannot tear off any more scales, it employs a new technique: it holds the cone firmly against the ground or branch, with one forepaw on the tip and the other on the scale-bearing section. It then begins to gnaw through the hard scales one by one and to eat the seeds. As the scales are in a helicoid position on the axis, the cone must be steadily turned while gnawing.

Squirrels do not normally gnaw off all of the scales, but leave the top ones like a little tuft at the top of the axis. Clearly it would be difficult for it to gnaw off these last few scales, as this is where it has hold of the cone with its paw. In addition, there are very few seeds in the top of the cone.

Depending on how close to the axis the ovuliferous scales have been gnawed off, the gnawed axes may have a thick, frayed appearance, or be thin, with a more even surface.

The gnawing-off of the hard ovuliferous scales leaves an oblique bitten surface, as one side edge of the remaining scale section is shorter than the other. It is always the case

Squirrel working on a spruce cone. The cone will end up as shown to the right in the drawing.

that the low edge is the side where the lower teeth entered. The high edge, where the teeth exited, generally ends in a little tip or point. Depending whether the squirrel held the cone's top end to the right or left while gnawing, these points will be on the left or right side of the gnawed surface, when the cone is positioned base downward.

As a particular squirrel will always hold a cone the same way, squirrels can be divided into right- or left-handed (a right-handed squirrel is one that holds the cone's top end to its right while gnawing, while a left-handed squirrel holds it the opposite way) (see drawing, page 131).

Young squirrels must learn to gnaw cones through experience. They begin fairly helplessly by gnawing here and there on the cone, but gradually they learn the correct technique.

When feeding on fragile cones with relatively thin scales, e.g. silver fir and larch cones, squirrels generally tear off all the scales except the little tuft at the top. While gnawing they hold the cone in their forepaws (see page 99).

Many pine cones are treated in a similar way, but squirrels can only tear apart unripe pine cones (possibly with the exception of the elongated cone of the Weymouth pine). They have to gnaw to pieces the ripe, highly lignified, solid cones. With arolla pine they have to gnaw their way through to each one of the large wingless seeds in these distinctive cones (see page 99).

In years with high seed production it is common to find cones on the ground that have not been completely gnawed by squirrels. These may have been discarded due to poor seed content, but generally they have been dropped while being gnawed up in a tree. Such cones may be finished off by other animals, with mice and birds often benefiting.

Mice and voles

Cones fed on by small rodents – primarily wood mice, yellow-necked mice and bank voles – are easy to distinguish from squirrel-gnawed cones, as the cone axis is always missing the basal tip characteristic of squirrel cones. This is because mice do not have the strength to tear off the basal scales, as squirrels can, but must gnaw them all in two. The basal ends of mouse-gnawed cones therefore have an even, rounded shape (see page 99).

Mice generally gnaw cones on the ground. They position themselves beside the cone and hold it with one forepaw on the gnawed-off axis and the other on the scale-covered section. The individual scales are normally not gnawed off entirely, but once the mouse is part way into the scale, it will tear it lengthways with a quick jerk of its head, tossing the gnawed-off piece aside. The thick scales of pine cones, however, are gnawed off entirely (see page 99). Once a scale has been removed the mouse turns the cone slightly with its forepaws so it can start gnawing the next scale in line. The exposed seeds are removed using its incisors, and it then releases the cone to hold the seed in its forepaws while eating it.

The gnawing-off is usually just at the point on the scale where the seeds are, and as the gnawed edges are not oblique like squirrels' but more or less straight, mouse-gnawed cones have a more regular and uniform appearance.

A wood mouse's cone workshop on the forest floor. The cones have a much smoother appearance than squirrel-gnawed cones (see photo, page 130).

Small rodents generally leave fewer top scales than squirrels, probably because they do not need as long a section to hold on to, and gnawed cones with all the top scales removed are fairly common.

Like squirrels, mice and voles may also be right- or left-handed, according to whether they hold the top end of the cone to their right or left while gnawing.

Cones gnawed by mice and voles are far

less commonly found than squirrel-gnawed cones. Unlike squirrels, they do not sit in the open when gnawing cones but find a hiding place under heaps of brushwood, tussocks etc. They may also manage to drag the cones down into their underground tunnels, where they can sit and eat in peace and quiet. The same feeding site is often used many times and may therefore have a considerable pile of gnawed cones.

Mice and voles are generally satisfied with the cones they are able to find on the forest floor, be these windfalls, cones from felled trees or those dropped by squirrels. However, you may occasionally see mountain pine cones, for example, that have been partially gnawed while still on the tree (see page 99).

Birds

Cones fed on by birds differ substantially in appearance from those attacked by rodents.

It is generally also easy to determine which species of bird has been at work – in the case of spruce and pine cones, which are mainly fed on by woodpeckers, crossbills and nutcrackers. Identification is much more difficult for the 'berries' of yew, which are fed on by many different small birds.

Great spotted woodpeckers: These birds feed largely on conifer seeds in winter. They peck the cone off the tree and fly with it in their beak to some crack or other, where they wedge it firmly, always tip upward. Using their chisel-shaped beak they set to work on the cone, pecking and prising the scales apart to get to the seeds. When one side is done, they loosen the cone and turn it round. A woodpecker's cone therefore has a very distinctive, ruffled appearance, with scales sticking out on all sides. Only the lower section of the cone is generally undamaged. The seeds, which are swallowed whole, are probably removed using their very long, sticky tongue. It takes around 4 minutes for a woodpecker to empty a pine cone of seeds, and in that short time it pecks at the cone approx. 800 times (see page 99).

Woodpeckers often choose a natural crack or crevice for securing their cone. The deep bark furrows on an old oak are ideal for this, and if there are plenty of furrows, each one is used only once. During the win-

Broken-up pine cones accumulating below a woodpecker's anvil in a pine tree. Note the cones wedged in the bark.

A woodpecker's anvil in a tree stump.

ter such trees can become completely orna-
mented with cones, giving them a very
strange appearance. The cones are wedged
very firmly, and can sometimes remain for
years.

Woodpeckers often make a groove for
the cone themselves using their beak. In this
instance the groove is used numerous times,
and the pecked cones accumulate below this
'anvil'. Once a cone is finished with, it is

usually left in the groove and only removed
once a fresh cone has been brought. You
would think it would be difficult for the
woodpecker to manoeuvre two cones at
once, but it manages very ingeniously by
wedging the new cone between its breast
and the trunk while it tosses the old one out
of the crack with its beak.

Crossbill: These distinctive coniferous
woodland birds are greatly dependent on

conifer seed production. They have a very unusual biology, as their breeding season falls between December and April, i.e. in midwinter. This is undoubtedly only possible due to the very calorie-rich conifer seeds (approx. 35% fat) that they specialise in eating, and which is the chicks' only food. Their breeding period coincides precisely with the period when the cones are mature and full of seeds.

Crossbills have an excellent tool for opening cones – their specially shaped beak. It is compressed and very powerful, and the

A parrot crossbill working on a pine cone. See also drawing below.

Three stages in crossbills' handling of cones. Left, it forces its beak in between the scales; centre, it twists it apart; and right, it removes the seed with its tongue.

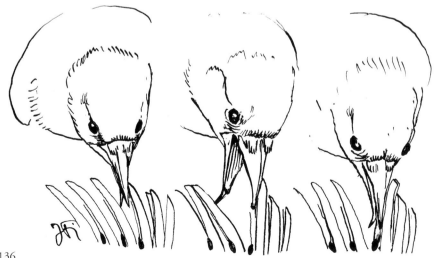

tips of both the upper and lower mandibles are elongated and curved, so they cross over. In some individuals the lower beak crosses to the left of the upper beak and in others to the right (left- or right-oriented).

Another distinctive characteristic of the crossbill is that the two mandibles articulate differently. One is a ball-and-socket joint, while the other allows substantial dislocation of the mandible to the side. For example, a right-oriented bird can only shift its mandible far enough to the left so that its beak tips are in a vertical line, but to the right it can shift it a full centimetre from the median plane.

When opening a cone, a crossbill always positions itself so that the tip of its lower mandible is turned in towards the cone. A left-oriented crossbill will therefore have the cone on its left side, while a right-oriented individual will have it to its right. It then opens its beak, and as it shifts its mandible until its beak tips are level, it turns its head and pushes its beak in under a scale. Once its beak has been pushed all the way in it closes it again, simultaneously shifting its mandible and turning its head. This manoeuvre lifts the scale, and the two seeds are released, to be captured by its tongue. As the beak closes or is pulled back, the scale is torn longitudinally, giving the cone a very distinctive appearance. However, the thick scales of pine cones are generally not split (see page 99). If you have ever tried to bend back a scale on a Norway spruce cone, you will realise how strong this bird actually is.

Common crossbills prefer Norway spruce, silver fir, sitka spruce, larch and mountain pine cones, but parrot crossbills, which have a much more powerful beak, also like the very strong Scots pine cones.

They usually bite off the cone and work on it perched on a branch, holding it firmly with one foot. However, common crossbills feed on Norway spruce cones while they are still attached to the tree.

Crossbills often appear in flocks, and you can generally spot them by the shower of seed wings and cones falling from a foraging flock. Crossbill visits are particularly easy to track in snow.

Nutcrackers: Forage frequently on the distinctive cones of lodgepole pine, pecking the large seeds to pieces. Many feed on yew 'berries', eating either the hard seed or the red aril.

Thrush: Often swallows yew 'berries' whole; however, it only digests the aril, the hard seed simply passing through, thus assisting the tree's seed dispersal.

Nuthatch: Also very keen on yew seeds, which it feeds on after having wedged them in a bark crack (see page 99).

Marsh tit: Takes yew 'berries' and flies carries them in its beak to a suitable feeding site on a level branch nearby. It squeezes the seed out of the aril, which is sticky and usually catches on the branch. Once the bird has removed the seed, it allows the empty case to fall to the ground (see page 99).

Hawfinch: Hawfinches also eat yew seeds. They can easily split the thick scales with a thrust of their large, powerful beak. When a flock of hawfinches has foraged in a yew, the ground below the tree will be completely dotted with ovuliferous scales and red arils. These feeding remains are naturally particularly conspicuous on snow (see page 99).

Hazelnuts

Hazelnuts are one of the most sought-after of all nuts, and are particularly prized by numerous rodents and birds.

However, the thick, hard shell makes it difficult for the animals to get to the actual kernel. It often takes a great deal of effort, and it is interesting to see the different methods they have developed and the various techniques that are used to open the nuts.

Their work on the nuts leaves clear marks in the form of beak and toothmarks. Due to the smooth, brown surface of the shells these marks are often very distinct and well defined. It is therefore easy to tell whether it is a bird or an animal with teeth that has been at the nut. With a little

Squirrel-gnawed hazelnut.

Bottom left, yellow-necked mouse/wood mouse; right, bank vole type.

practice you will also often be able to identify the species concerned with complete accuracy.

Squirrel

Squirrels are major nut-eaters. They use a method equivalent to cutting the tip off with a knife, pushing the knife-blade into the crack and twisting it so the shell bursts.

The squirrel holds the nut firmly in its forepaws and gnaws an incision across the tip so a small opening appears, into which it sticks its lower incisors, and using them as a jemmy, breaks the shell into pieces. The pieces of shell, scattered on the ground below the tree where the squirrel has fed, are easy to identify and cannot really be confused with nuts fed on by other animals.

Squirrels learn from experience how best to open the nuts. Young squirrels gnaw random incisions all over the nut, until by chance a hole appears, into which they can insert their lower teeth and break a piece of shell off. They gradually learn the most effective way to gnaw (see page 100).

Sometimes squirrels take nuts that are not yet ripe. The soft shell allows them to easily bite off the top of the nut, and then fish out the little, undeveloped kernel with their lower incisors, which, as with mice, can be used as pincers (see page 100).

Like so many other rodents, in autumn, when food is plentiful, squirrels may hide away a reserve. This usually consists of beechnuts, acorns and nuts, which are buried or tucked at random into nooks and crannies, either individually or in little batches. Occasionally they may have actual stores with a major cache. There seems to be little method involved in such hoarding,

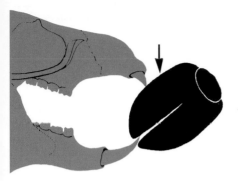

The squirrel's method of opening a hazelnut. Its lower incisors are inserted into the hole that has first been gnawed in the tip of the nut (see photograph, page 140). With its upper teeth it then presses the nut down so that it splits.

and it is frequently pure chance if the hidden food is found again. However, squirrel tracks in the snow have often been found to lead directly to a spot where a cache was buried. In these instances there is no doubt that the squirrel knew exactly where the reserves were.

A squirrel working on a hazelnut.

Mice and voles

When feeding on hazelnuts, the various species of small rodent begin in the same basic way. They find a spot on the surface of the nut with a bump or groove to act as an anchor for their upper incisors (see page 112), and they then scrape rapidly and loosely at the shell with their lower incisors.

The different species vary in where on the nut they prefer to begin. Some generally start from one of the ends, while others gnaw in from the side. Water voles almost always gnaw from the side, while bank voles

and striped field mice gnaw from the end. In a survey in Germany, of 1,309 hazelnuts gnawed by yellow-necked mice 46.8 % were opened from the side, while only 10.1 % of 628 nuts gnawed by wood mice were opened that way.

Until the rodent has got through the shell and made a hole in the nut, the gnawing marks of the various species look practically identical, and it is generally almost im-

Nut hoard of wood mouse in an old rotten beech.

possible to identify the species from the gnawing alone. Theoretically you should be able to identify the gnawing by measuring the width of the toothmarks on the nuts and comparing them with measurements taken directly from the rodent.

However, the lower incisors of all our small rodents are extremely pointed, which means they leave marks of more or less the same width and appearance. In addition, the two lower jaw halves are not firmly fixed and are therefore very mobile in relation to one another. The distance between the two teeth is therefore not constant when gnawing.

Toothmarks from the upper incisors are more useful in this respect, but the marks are often on top of one another and so close that it is impossible to obtain accurate measurements.

As soon as the small rodent has made a hole in the nut, it begins to eat, pulling pieces of the kernel out using its lower inci-

sors. It generally then holds the extracted kernel fragments in its forepaws while eating. The great mobility of the two lower jaw halves serves the animal well here, as the two long incisors can be used as a kind of pincers, to extricate the loosened pieces of kernel. When it cannot reach any more through the hole it begins gnawing again, widening the hole evenly on all sides.

In its efforts to get the kernel out it often sticks its lower teeth so far into the hole that the upper incisors scrape the outside of the nut, leaving long, light scratches on it.

Mice and voles usually eat at special feeding spots, well hidden under a tussock, some brushwood or similar, where they can sit in peace and quiet. At such spots you may find large quantities of gnawed nuts.

Some small rodents use nuts as a winter cache. In autumn, water voles gather large quantities in their underground tunnel system, where they feed on them during the winter. The empty shells are carried out the following autumn, when the store is being refilled, and left in large piles outside the holes leading down to the tunnel system.

While all mice and voles, as mentioned, begin working on nuts in the same way, it is interesting that once they have made a hole in the nut, they divide into two groups each with their own gnawing technique, which leaves differing marks. The two types of gnawing are described as the wood mouse type and the bank vole type after the species from which they were initially identified.

Wood mouse type: When gnawing, wood mice hold the nut pressed against the ground with their forelegs, so it is tilted in towards their breast. Once they have made a hole in the shell, they stick their lower incisors into the hole, and, resting their upper incisors against the outside of the shell, they gnaw at the edge of the hole facing away from their body. So the gnawing is from within outwards, and as the mouse turns the nut round as it gnaws the upper incisors leave a series of marks on the outside just below the edge of the hole, often in the form of a groove, which appear very distinctly as light marks on the brown shell (see page 100). Yellow-necked mice, bank voles and dormice gnaw like wood mice. Water voles, which are rat sized, have a very powerful bite, however, so the gnawed edge is therefore irregular and serrated. On thin-shelled nuts their gnawing looks almost like a fracture.

Bank vole type: Bank voles also hold the nut pressed against the ground with their forelegs, but, unlike wood mice, they hold the nut below them with the base under their breast and the tip tilted forward away from them. Once they have made a hole in

the nut, unlike wood mice they stick their nose into the hole and gnaw at the nearest edge. So the gnawing is from the outside in, and the gnawed edge is sharp on the undamaged exterior. The marks left by the upper incisors on the inside of the shell protrude slightly due to the loose, brown layer covering the inside of the shell (see page 100).

Although the striped field mouse is closely related to the wood mouse and yellow-necked mouse, it gnaws hazelnuts in the same way as the bank vole. Nuts fed on by dormice have a very regular hole, and the toothmarks are so faint that the gnawed edge is almost completely smooth (see page 100).

Two different ways of handling hazelnuts by small rodents. See text for further details.

Wood mouse

Bank vole

141

Birds

Birds open nuts by pecking the shell to pieces. As it generally takes several pecks before the shell breaks, hazelnuts fed on by birds will usually have numerous peck and beak marks, which are clearly visible on the smooth, brown surface. Since the beak tips of nut-eating birds differ in shape, you can sometimes identify the bird that fed on the nut, based on the appearance of the beak marks.

Great spotted woodpeckers: The beak tips of great spotted woodpeckers are compressed and chisel-shaped, and leave marks approx. 2 mm long (see page 100).

To keep a nut secure while working on it, woodpeckers wedge it into some kind of crack. This could be a naturally-occurring crack in an old post, a bark crevice or similar, but it often hews out a niche itself, that is just the right size for a nut. This kind of feeding site is called a woodpecker 'anvil',

and as these are generally used for long periods, there will usually be numerous broken nutshells on the ground below.

The structure of nutshells means that they split most easily longitudinally – and woodpeckers know how to exploit this. Nuts are always placed base downward, and the pecking is done in a line lengthways along the nut, following the same principle as a stonemason splitting a block.

Nuthatch: Nuthatches' beak marks are crescent-shaped and therefore easy to distinguish from those of woodpeckers. Only the upper beak leaves marks, as it protrudes slightly further than the lower beak (see page 100).

They wedge the nut in a natural bark crevice, which is only used once. Once the nut is empty it is usually left there, and so there are no piles of empty nutshells below nuthatch 'anvils'.

Nuthatches, which are smaller than most

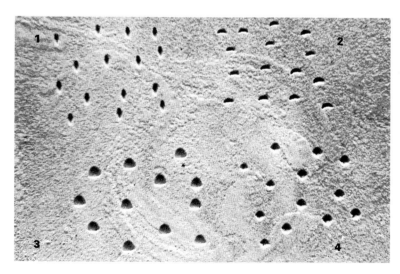

Beak marks.
1: Woodpecker.
2: Nuthatch.
3: Magpie.
4: Great tit.

A hazelnut fed on by a great spotted wood-pecker, wedged in a bark crack.

A hazelnut fed on by a nuthatch, wedged in a bark hole.

woodpeckers, are not able to split the nut in the same way, but have to peck a roundish hole in the side of the nut.

In late summer and autumn, nuthatches stockpile various types of seed, hiding them in bark crevices and similar places, to serve as food during the winter. Hazelnuts are particularly popular for this. Nuthatches do not keep close track of their hiding-places, but, unlike most other birds, they also maintain their territories in winter, so it is probable that the birds that find the seeds in

winter are the same ones that hid them in autumn.

Magpie: Magpies' beak tips are shaped almost like a low three-sided pyramid with convex sides, and leave a relatively large, round mark on nuts. Like nuthatches, only the tip of the upper mandible leaves marks. They usually work on nuts on the ground, holding them with one foot (see page 100).

Great tit: The great tit's beak marks resemble those of a magpie, but are much smaller, and as the upper and lower mandibles protrude equally, the whole beak tip has a slightly quadrangular shape. This shape is difficult to see, however, in the peck marks on nuts. Great tits prefer almost ripe nuts with relatively soft shells (see page 100). **Nutcracker**: As their name suggests, nutcrackers are very keen nut-eaters, and when possible they collect and bury them for winter. Their pecking is very powerful and usually at the tip of the nut, so it splits in two. However, thin-shelled nuts are often pecked to pieces from the side. They work on nuts at a particular feeding site, a tree stump or similar, securing them with one foot (see page 100).

Walnuts

Walnuts are highly valued by many animals, and it is common to find gnawed examples.

The walnut's very hard shell with its gnarled surface means that teeth and beak marks are rarely visible, making it difficult to determine what animal has fed on it.

Animals rarely have difficulty making holes in the nuts, as they have a couple of thin-walled sections near the tip that are easy to break through.

Rodents

Squirrel: Squirrels open walnuts by forcing their lower incisors in through one of the thin-walled sections. Using their teeth as a jemmy they then burst the shells open. If it is not possible to force their teeth through the shell, they make a hole by gnawing a deep groove in it.

Mice and voles: They do not have the strength to burst the shells and must there-

fore laboriously gnaw their way in to the kernel. They often, but not always, begin by gnawing at the thin-walled sections and produce very uniform gnawing that is easy to recognise by the numerous fine toothmarks from the lower incisors (see page 100).

Birds

Great tit: These small birds can only peck out the thin sections of the shell and must therefore be satisfied with as much of the kernel as they can get at through the rather uniformly pecked holes. Great tits usually work on nuts while they are still on the tree. However, these will often fall and the birds may then complete their work on the ground (see page 100).

Jackdaw: Jackdaws usually take walnuts straight from the tree and transport them to a feeding site on the ground or a branch. They hold the nut firmly against the ground or branch with one foot, pecking a large, irregular hole in it with their powerful beak. There are generally no clear beak marks visible on the shells (see page 100).

Crossbill: In years with poor spruce seed production crossbills may attack walnuts. However, they can only cope with very thin-shelled or unripe nuts, and simply bite the shells to pieces on both sides of the strong ridge (see page 100).

Beechnuts and acorns

Beechnuts and acorns are the fruits of the beech and oak respectively. Their shells are not as strong as those of hazelnuts and walnuts.

Rodents

Beechnuts and acorns are very popular with small rodents, especially wood mice and yellow-necked mice, and gnawed shell remains are common at their feeding sites in beech and oak woodland. Marks from the incisors are clearly visible on the gnawed edges of the shells, as they give the edge an uneven, scalloped appearance.

They open beechnuts by either gnawing away two of the three edges, so one side of the shell falls off and the kernel can be removed, or by gnawing away the broad bottom of the shell, so the kernel can be pulled out. On acorns they usually begin by gnawing a hole in the broad base, which is uneven, allowing their teeth to grip easily (see page 101).

Piles of beechnuts outside a wood mouse's hole.

Birds

You can often find pecked remains of beechnuts wedged in bark cracks. Birds place them there in order to peck the kernel out. As there are generally no clear beak marks, it is difficult to determine what bird it was, but it is most often woodpeckers or nuthatches. You may also frequently see intact beechnuts in cracks in the bark; these are nuthatch winter caches, waiting to be eaten.

In winter, flocks of finches – especially *bramblings* and *greenfinches* – often forage on the ground in beech woodland. If you look more closely, you will find they were eating beechnuts; there will be small piles of broken shells mixed with small, white kernel fragments, the remains of beech 'mast'.

Cherries and plums

The fleshy fruits of cherry and plum trees are sought after by many animals; some eat the entire fruit, while others are happy with either the flesh or the kernels.

Mammals that eat cherries whole include foxes and badgers. Martens frequently take fallen plums, but may also take the fruits on the trees. Birds include blackheaded gulls and various members of the crow family. All these animals actually only digest the flesh, and the stones remain intact in the pellets or droppings. There will be no marks on such seeds to give clues to the animal's species. Identification can be made from the additional content and the form of the droppings or pellets (see page 177 and 205).

Rodents

Squirrel: Squirrels generally just eat the flesh, but sometimes gnaw on the stones. **Mice and voles:** It is mainly the stones which are attacked, and their gnawing is easy to recognise by its regularity and the numerous toothmarks, visible as fine grooves along the gnawed edge. On both plum and cherry stones you can distinguish between the same two types of gnawing as mentioned under hazelnuts (page 141): *wood mouse type*, with clear toothmarks along the gnawed edge, and *bank vole type*, which lacks these toothmarks (see page 101).

Birds

Starlings and thrushes: These birds are often seen foraging in cherry trees, so a description is unnecessary. They eat only the flesh, and you can often see stones that have been picked clean still on their stalks.
Hawfinch: Hawfinches are also keen cherry-eaters. They do not eat the flesh but pick out the stone, crack it with their extremely powerful beak and then eat the kernel. There are no beak marks visible on the stones, but they are split in a distinctive way into two equal sized halves, usually lying side by side on the ground together with the remains of the cherry. In winter hawfinches may search the ground under cherry trees for the stones, and if you look, you can find the broken remains. Hawfinches treat plum stones, sloe stones and many other hard-shelled seeds in the same manner (see page 101).

Rosehips

Rosehips are the fruits of roses. They have a fleshy skin and inside this a quantity of nutrient-rich achenes.

Rodents

The small rosehip nuts (achenes) are eaten by *squirrels* and *mice*. As squirrels find it difficult to sit and eat up on the thorny rose branches, their feeding sites are generally on the ground. Squirrels crack the nut longitudinally, while mice gnaw in from the broad, basal end and pull the kernel out (see page 101).

Birds

In winter the red, fleshy part of rosehips is important for many birds, particularly the

Rowan berries are a popular food for birds such as tits.

various thrush species. They are only interested in the flesh and leave the many small nuts behind; however, the opposite is true of finches. They peck away the flesh, leaving small fragments scattered on branches and leaves, and eat the kernels, after having cracked open the nuts with their beak.

Apples

Rodents
Feeding signs made by small rodents can frequently be seen on apples – both in the wild and in gardens. In most cases they eat both the flesh and the pips, and the gnawing is easily recognisable by the many small toothmarks along the gnawed edge of the skin, and by the oblong depressions the lower incisors make in the flesh. It is often difficult to identify the animal *species* by the gnawing alone. However, you can always determine from the size of the toothmarks whether it was done by a large rodent (squirrel, rat or water vole) or small rodent (mouse or vole), as toothmarks of the former are almost twice as large as those of the latter. Exact identification can only be made with the help of other signs, location etc.

Birds
Many birds eat apples, but by far the most common signs are those left by thrushes. They can be seen particularly on windfall apples, but also on those still on the tree.

Greenfinches peck out the seeds from shrivelled rosehips.

Rosehips fed on by greenfinches.

Hawfinch eating apple pips.

These birds are only interested in the flesh and work around the core. They take as little as possible of the skin, so the apple is hollowed out, leaving a bowl shape with the core in the centre. On the inside of the bowl marks from the pointed beak are clearly visible.

Unlike thrushes, crossbills tackle apples for their pips. Due to their specially-shaped beak (see page 136) apples fed on by crossbills have a very distinctive appearance. As they literally gnaw their way in to the core, they bite out pieces of flesh, which often remain attached to the apple in small clusters. Crossbills prefer small apple varieties such as Siberian crab or wild apples, as these have many pips and less flesh to bite through.

Wild boar can cause major damage in maize fields.

Cereals

The various cultivated cereals attract many animals, whose foraging on crops can cause significant damage, with major financial consequences.

Badger
Oat fields may be visited by badgers, which like to eat unripe cereals. Their technique is to pull the stems down with their forelegs, then strip off the oats.

Deer
In fields bordered by forest stands it is common for deer to venture in at dusk or early in the morning and bite off or pluck the ears of cereals in a belt along the forest fringe. This often happens while the cereals are still totally unripe.

Rodents
Maize fields are frequently attacked by rats and mice, which climb up the plants and gnaw off the soft grains in the ears after hav-

ing gnawed off the large spathes, on which the toothmarks are clearly visible.

Small rodents' feeding signs are easy to recognise on ripe, dry maize grains, as they mainly eat the soft seed section, giving the nibbled kernels a distinctive crescent-shaped appearance (see page 101).

Apart from individual species such as the harvest mouse, most small rodents are too heavy to climb up among the more thin-stalked cereals, so to get to the ears they first fell the straw by gnawing through it at ground level. They then gnaw off the ear and drag it to a suitable feeding site. House mice and rats gnaw oat grains in different ways, so identification is always easy. *House mice* gnaw the grains from the side, holding the ends with their forepaws, and leaving oblong flakes. *Rats* gnaw the grains from

Field voles are one of the major cereal-eaters.

Maize attacked by rats.

one end, however, so the remains consist of large and small end pieces (see page 101).

Birds

Fields of cereals, particularly those close to towns, are visited by *flocks of sparrows,* which in the worst instances can completely strip the seeds from the ears. They begin by eating the lowest seeds and steadily work their way up the ear. Many of the straws break under the birds' weight, and the field is left looking untidy.

151

Sparrows also forage frequently on ears of maize, but they leave the spathes behind, often ragged and torn.

Other seeds

As all types of seeds can serve as food for animals, feeding sites with seed remains are often found in the countryside. For example, when *redpolls* pull seeds out of thistle heads, or when *siskins* forage on catkins, or when *great tits* help themselves to rowan berries, the snow around the feeding sites will be sprinkled with plant residue. *Mice* generally bite the seed heads off and take them to a feeding site, where remains can be found piled together. Wood mice and yellow-necked mice bite off catkins up in the trees and bring them down to the ground before feeding.

Beet

Beet fields are excellent for spotting feeding signs, as many different animals are interested in the juicy vegetables, and the feeding signs are usually very distinct and easily recognisable.

Deer
Deer often visit beet fields. *Red deer,* for example, pull the plants up long before the

Young siskin enjoying some thistle seeds.

Beet gnawed by water vole (left), hare (centre) and fallow deer (right).

beet is fully-grown, and as they only take a single bite from each beet and leave the rest, they destroy much more than they eat. They generally only eat the above-ground parts of full-grown beet, and the marks from their large lower incisors are visible as wide, one-sided grooves on the beet's surface.

Hares and rodents

Hares also like to gnaw beet, and, like deer species, they often eat only a little of each. As they also only eat part of what they bite off, they always damage an excessively large number of plants. Due to the groove at the front of their upper incisors (see page 112), the toothmarks are easily recognisable: the gnawing looks as if it has been done by an animal with four narrow upper teeth and two large lower teeth.

When *water voles* gnaw beet, they always do so from below, gnawing their way into the beet under the ground and hollowing it out, leaving only a thin husk. Bank voles

like to eat the entire beet before starting on the next one, which is more acceptable from the farmer's point of view. When *rats* gnaw beet, they begin from the top and gnaw their way down into the beet, hollowing it out and leaving a deep bowl.

Herbaceous plants

Herbaceous plants are a very important food source for a large number of animals. For large herbivores such as deer, and for many rodents, the leaves or roots of these plants are their most important food all year round. Some of them, however, e.g. many gamebirds, only eat herbaceous plants at certain times of the year.

Feeding signs on herbaceous plants are generally not very conspicuous and are often difficult or impossible to identify accurately. Certain distinctive features are in evidence, however, for the various animal groups, and collating these with other signs such as

153

droppings and footprints, combined with a little knowledge about the animals found in the locality in question, will generally allow correct identification.

A roe deer has scraped the snow away to get to the herbaceous vegetation. Compare the photo on page 223.

Deer

Deer feeding signs are seldom noticeable in summer, as deer rarely graze heavily on plants but eat a little here and there as they go. In winter, however, their feeding sites stand out very clearly, as they scrape the snow aside with their forehooves to get to the herbaceous vegetation below.

Reindeer prefer to forage on lichen-rich areas below the timberline in winter. In good foraging conditions there will be very little evidence that reindeer have been there. However, if conditions are poor, with deep snow, the foraging will be concentrated, and the lichen covering gnawed off in winding bands, which may remain visible for many years.

Rodents

Among small rodents, *voles* (see page 52) in particular feed on herbaceous plants. Along field vole and water vole trails you will always find feeding sites with remains of gnawed leaves and stems. As they like to be sheltered while eating, their feeding sites are always under cover of some sort, a clump of grass, a fallen log or similar. After the snow melts, in early spring, one may often find seemingly fresh field vole feeding sites out in the open, but these can be explained. When in use these were underneath the snow, and the low temperature and high humidity kept the food remains and droppings fresh, making them look like active spring sites.

The feeding sites are often a little way away from the gnawed plant, but if you lift the drooping blades of grass, you will often see where the lowest and juiciest parts of the outer shoots of the tussock have been gnawed away by field voles, while the upper

Soft-rush gnawed by a field vole. Only the green parts of the stems are eaten.

section, with the blades, is still in place. While foraging they create a well-trodden path full of droppings around the foot of the tussock.

Marks from the animal's teeth are generally clearly visible on the gnawed plant matter at the feeding sites. The leaves will have a series of small, curved notches, and on long, narrow grass blades these will be transverse, as they are usually eaten from one end. In addition to food remains, large quantities of droppings are also always found at feeding sites.

Water vole and field vole feeding sites are similar, but are easy to distinguish from one another by size. Water voles often gnaw much larger plant matter than field voles, and their toothmarks are at least twice as large. Their droppings are also much larger (see page 178).

A particularly conspicuous and interesting feeding trace from field voles – and probably also bank voles – is frequently found on soft-rushes in winter. Rush stems are gnawed through at the bottom and divided into suitable lengths for the vole to hold in its forepaws while it gnaws off and eats the green outer layer. The spongy pith is left at the feeding site, its chalk-white colouring revealing the site from a distance.

155

In fields with winter crops, and especially in new alfalfa fields, you can frequently see where field voles have foraged on the green leaves under the snow and often completely gnawed them away in large sections of the field. Hares and deer also feed on these fields, but usually later, once the plants have grown more.

In autumn, water voles gather a winter cache, often consisting of juicy stemwood, swollen roots or bulbs. In spring you will often see thistles, dandelions and similar plants that are totally shrivelled. If you pull them up you will find that the thick, juicy roots have been gnawed away. Many gardeners have bitter experience of water vole activities: neatly arranged bulbs either not coming up at all or growing in a clump from an abandoned water vole cache. The gnawed stemwood and bulbs will usually show clear marks from the animal's teeth.

Birds

Many birds – especially gamebirds – feed mainly on fresh, green leaves in spring, and their beak marks can be seen as sharp, wedge-shaped notches in the leaves.

Most gardeners are familiar with *sparrows* foraging on crocus flowers. They are primarily after the stamens, but they also feed on the petals, where their beak marks are clearly visible. Oddly enough, house sparrows much prefer yellow crocuses, but they do also take the others.

Geese and some *duck species* are often seen grazing on fields of winter crops, biting off the fresh shoots and leaves. In parks mallards may bite off crocus shoots in spring, just as they are emerging from the soil. They sometimes eat the shoots right down to the bulb, boring a hole approximately 5 cm deep with their beak, which superficially may resemble a mouse hole.

Animal remains

Remains found at the feeding sites of predators are usually called 'prey', particularly when they are from a warm-blooded creature.

If it is small, a mouse or a small bird for example, it will generally be swallowed in its entirety, perhaps after having been pulled apart, and there will be nothing left at the feeding site but a tuft of fur, a couple of feathers or a little blood. However, if the prey is large, there will often be quite a lot remaining, and it is possible to determine, from such evidence as toothmarks, which animal caught it. Based on this alone, however, it is quite difficult, and often impossible, to identify a predator from its feeding

Pygmy owl in flight with its prey, a mouse.

site. Generally the location of the feeding site, footprints, droppings and so on may help, but even then an accurate identification can be difficult. Identification is made harder by the fact that it is common for the same prey item to be used by several different predators. The remains of a hare, for example, on the feeding site of a large bird of prey will often have been visited by crows and gulls; foxes, various small rodents and shrews often exploit these opportunities too.

It really cannot be assumed that an animal whose remains are found at a predator's feeding site was actually killed by it. This is something that many hunters in particular forget when they judge the harmfulness of a particular predator. Predators often go for whatever is easiest to get hold of, and so in winter, many of them feed on carrion, which can remain fresh over long periods due to the low temperatures.

For most people, there is something infinitely fascinating about predators. In addition to their beautiful appearance, it is probably the fact that they feed on other animals that makes them so interesting. There is also a certain special feeling when you look at a predator's feeding site and learn from it about that particular animal's feeding choices, its way of eating, and perhaps about its method of hunting.

Predatory mammals

It is actually rather rare to find the feeding remains of predatory mammals. As mentioned previously, small prey will be eaten whole. Larger prey will generally be dragged

to a relatively hidden feeding site, and their remains will be buried or covered with leaves, moss or snow – a phenomenon familiar to us from the burying of bones by dogs.

The prey is often dragged to the animal's home, so a good place for finding many different prey remains is outside the entrance of an inhabited fox burrow. Organic matter added to the earth in this way will, together with droppings and urine, act as fertiliser, and you can clearly see how the growth of vegetation around the entrance to an old fox burrow is often considerably lusher than that further away. Even plant species especially demanding of nutrients can grow here. Where a beech marten is living in a loft or a shed, you can also see remains of its prey. These are primarily birds, but it is not uncommon to find eggshells and the remains of hedgehogs, with almost everything eaten except for the skin with all the spines attached.

Remains of birds

Predatory mammals deal with birds in quite a characteristic way, and their remains are generally easy to recognise from similar remains at the feeding sites of birds of prey (see page 164).

The brain is clearly a particular delicacy, so the head is bitten off and eaten first. Then the body feathers are bitten off in clumps, more or less stuck together with saliva. The larger feathers show clear signs of having been bitten, often missing the bottom part of the quill, which will end up in the predator's droppings. The tips of the wings are bitten off, or the primaries themselves are bitten off so close to the wing

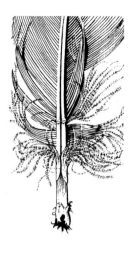

Feathers left after predators' attacks. The feather on the left shows traces of attack by a mammal (a stoat); the quill has been bitten. The one on the right was the work of a bird of prey; the quill is intact – the feather was torn out. Beak marks are sometimes visible a little above the quill.

that they are only connected by a narrow strip of skin. The tail is dealt with in a similar way. The remains of the bird's bones show clear signs of being crushed or bitten.

Remains of mammals

Small dead mammals are seen relatively rarely in the wild, for, as stated earlier, they are quickly eaten by other animals. Shrews are an exception, however, and very often dead shrews can be seen lying in the middle of a path, on a tree stump or on a large stone. The reason for this is that shrews have a gland on each side of their bodies which produces a musky secretion disliked by many animals. On closer examination it can sometimes be seen that the dead shrew was killed by a carnivore, often a fox, a bird

A common sight: a dead shrew. The predator is unknown.

159

of prey or an owl. It was presumably mistaken for a mouse; the error first being discovered when it was too late for the shrew. However, some animals do eat shrews; one of these is the barn owl, which often specialises in catching them.

Small rodents are very important for many of the smaller predatory mammals, and although they are generally eaten whole, fur and skin included, feeding sites are sometimes betrayed in other ways. It is thus common to see on fields and slopes signs that a fox has dug up nests of field voles or water voles and taken all the young, leaving behind the plaited hay nesting materials amongst the debris. The fox identifies the nest by sound or smell.

The various *large carnivores* each handle their prey in their own way when it concerns other large mammals. By observing the carcase and surroundings of the feeding site, you can often gain indications as to which animal has been active. It is also always important to look for footprints, fur and droppings.

However, it must be noted that there is a degree of overlap in the behaviour of the various species and also that most carnivores will gladly eat animals that have died of natural causes or have been killed by other animals.

Bear: bears often kill their prey with a blow from their front paws. This causes bruising, which can be seen if the carcase is pulled apart. The blows will generally be directed towards areas where the spine will break.

Another very characteristic technique is nose-biting. Occasionally there are clear, deep signs of canines to be seen (the distance between the canines is 45-65 mm).

The whole of the front of the skull may be crushed. The nose-bite is probably primarily intended to shock the prey into collapsing. However, other carnivores may also use nose-biting, and creatures such as foxes, eagles and ravens can feed on the nose area in a way that is reminiscent of a bear's bite.

Finally, it must be mentioned that bears also sometimes use neck-bites to kill their prey.

The bear often begins its feed at the breast or hip areas; the entrails are also eaten early on. The bones are pulled apart and usually crushed by the bear's powerful jaws before being eaten.

The bear's hoarding behaviour is highly characteristic. The prey is laid on a suitable surface, and up to several cubic metres of moss, heather and earth is pulled up to cover the carcase. In spring snow is often used instead. Bears also store items in streams.

A large deer, for example, constitutes a resource that the bear can come back to again and again. In such cases there will also be a number of signs surrounding the prey. There may be droppings, resting sites, excavated anthills, and characteristically, broken-off and chewed twigs and small whole trees snapped (the reason for this curious behaviour is unknown).

Wolverine: the killing method seems to be rather stereotypical. Like the lynx (see page 161), it jumps onto the back of its prey, but because of its different build it is unable to reach the throat. Instead it attempts to kill its prey with a rapid bite to the neck. In extreme cases the vertebrae are crushed by the wolverine's powerful jaws. Normally it only takes a few bites, while foxes and

Sheep killed by a wolverine.

dogs etc. usually need to take repeated bites. The distance between the canines is 25-35 mm.

If the wolverine is not able to kill its prey immediately, there will often be clear signs of a struggle.

The wolverine typically divides the prey up. The head, limbs and entrails are carried away for storage in suitable pieces, often over long distances. It usually buries the prey in snow, if possible, or in hollows under rocks or large stones, or in streams. It occasionally stores them in trees, but this appears to be less common than was once thought.

Lynx: the lynx's method of killing its prey also seems to be fairly stereotypical. It jumps up onto the animal's back, and usually manages to kill it with a precise bite to the throat. The victim probably suffocates – though shock may also play a part.

The signs of the throat-bite can often be confirmed by closer examination of the throat and windpipe. In some cases the fine holes made by the lynx's sharp canines can only be seen if the throat and windpipe are slit open. The distance between the canines is 25-35 mm.

If the lynx is unable to reach the throat, it will on occasion use a neck-bite, but never leaves bites down the back, as are often seen after a wolverine's attack.

There are rarely signs of a struggle at a spot where a lynx has made a kill.

A lynx has killed this reindeer with a bite to the throat.

The lynx seems to begin its meal with the shoulder and the thigh. The head and the upper part of the throat are left untouched, as are the lungs and stomach.

The lynx does not normally store food, but on occasion it partially covers the remains of a prey, particularly the open wounds.

The lynx seldom goes for carrion.

Wolf: the method of attack can vary from prey to prey, and also depends on whether the prey attempts to defend itself or flees. So it will attack large deer from behind, as far away as possible from the front hooves, while smaller animals are often attacked at the front. The distance between the canines is 35-50mm.

If wolves attack in packs, as they usually do, the prey may be badly mauled during the killing, with many wounds and gashes.

The wolf often seems to begin feeding at the prey's open wounds. If there are several wolves together, the feeding will be quite unsystematic. Each wolf can eat several kilos of flesh at a time, so if there are many of them, soon all that will be left is just a few gnawed bones and some skin.

Sometimes the wolf will hide away parts of the kill. After eating its fill, it may gnaw off some flesh, which is carried away. It then digs a flat hollow, places the flesh in it, and nudges earth over it with its snout, as dogs do. In winter it may bury the kill in snow instead.

If the prey is large, wolves stay in the vicinity until it is all eaten. In such cases there will be downtrodden resting places around the kill, with a lot of droppings and wolf fur.

It can be difficult to distinguish between the killing and feeding methods of wolves and dogs.

Fox: the fox seems to bite any part of the animal it is attacking, but will try to reach the neck to kill it. The fox's teeth and jaws are relatively small and weak in comparison with those of larger carnivores, so animals killed by foxes will have a large number of small perforations to the skin, unlike the large holes, gashes and other injuries inflicted by large carnivores. The distance between the canines is 20-25 mm.

The fox is not an efficient killer of larger animals, and the fight can last a long time. The spot is therefore often well trampled, with blood and bits of fur scattered about.

The fox does not appear to have a fixed pattern as to what it eats first. It frequently gnaws the head off and carries this away. It is also typical for it to take the entrails to bury them or give them to its young. This is also, however, common in wolverines and is sometimes seen in wolves.

Marten: the various species of marten kill large prey with a bite to the neck, usually just behind the head. Small animals such as small rodents are killed by a bite to the head itself. Sometimes martens kill far more animals than they want to eat or drag away. This can be seen in pigeon-houses or hen-houses, for example, and has given rise to the belief that martens can suck blood from their victims – this is, however, simply not true. Foxes can cause similar blood-baths in colonies of brooding gulls.

Remains of amphibians and fish

Otter: at otters' feeding sites by the banks of rivers and lakes, you can almost always find remains of fish, their main source of food, though they also catch crayfish and frogs. The otter usually eats the fish's head first, often leaving part of the tail.

A fallow deer's carcase, gnawed by foxes.

An otter's feeding site, with empty shells.

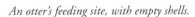

Seal: fishermen sometimes find that seals have attacked fish they have caught on their lines. Often there is only part of the head left on the hook.

Polecat: the polecat is a keen hunter of amphibians, and at its feeding sites in damp areas and on lakeshores you can find remains of frogs and toads. Toads' heads are often left behind – probably because they contain large poison glands – and as they are killed with a bite to the head, the marks of the polecat's teeth can be seen on it.

Mink: mink primarily live near water, hunting fish and small mammals. Large quantities of fish scales can be seen at its feeding sites, particularly in winter.

At a mink's feeding site you may find fish scales and fins.

Birds of prey

In contrast to the feeding sites of predatory mammals, those of birds of prey are very conspicuous, particularly when the prey was a bird; they are also very common, and are easily spotted in the wild. Birds of prey handle their victims very differently from predatory mammals (see page 158), so it is generally quite simple to determine which of the two kinds of predator has used the feeding site. However, it must be remembered that several different animals can pick at the same prey.

An exception is the feeding sites of *owls,* where there are few remains or none at all. Birds are plucked only partially, usually up in the trees, and small rodents are swallowed whole or divided into only a few pieces. The

many indigestible bits of owls' food, such as feathers, fur and bones, are found in their pellets (see page 209). The eagle owl leaves partial meal remains; but this owl is so big – Europe's largest owl – that it can overpower prey as large as a hare.

Remains of birds

When a bird of prey has caught a bird, it usually tears its head off first and eats the brain, which, as previously mentioned, is a particular delicacy, while the beak and skull remains are left lying at the feeding site. The head is not always eaten, however; sometimes it lies untouched with the other remains of the meal.

Next it begins to pluck the kill, pulling the feathers out with its beak, so gradually the feeding site is covered with down and feathers, blown out in a long strip away from the feeding site by the wind. The larger feathers are pulled out individually, leaving the quills undamaged, in contrast to what happens at the feeding sites of predatory mammals. If you examine the feathers carefully you can often see where the bird of prey grasped it with its beak. Sometimes the feather is actually cracked at that point.

Of the body itself, it is usually the breast musculature that is eaten first. The bird's sharp beak tears wedge-shaped pieces out of the crest of the breastbone, making some very characteristic incisions, which are always a sure sign that the kill was the victim of a bird of prey. The birds do not eat the larger bones, though smaller bone fragments are swallowed, to be coughed up in pellets later, together with small feathers and down which they were unable to avoid eating. The

intestines and stomach are not normally eaten, and close examination will reveal these lying on the feeding site together with the legs.

The plucking site will naturally look different depending on whether the prey was eaten there or plucked there but devoured at another spot. If it is eaten at that spot, there will be remains of feathers, beak, intestinal tract etc., and parts of the skeleton itself.

In the breeding season, many birds pluck their prey some distance from the nest to avoid disclosing its whereabouts; then they bring it to their brooding mate or to the young. Therefore, plucking sites of this kind will not contain the skeleton.

△ *Owls sometimes wedge their prey in the angle of a branch.*

A duck at a goshawk's plucking site. The ruptured breast can clearly be seen. ▽

A sparrowhawk has swooped down, probably onto a small bird. The wing marks point to a short struggle before the hawk rose again with its prey.

When the birds in the nest have finished with the kill, the remains are taken away and discarded at random. Only towards the end of the breeding season, when the birds have grown less cautious, are the remains thrown out over the edge of the nest; then there are a lot of picked-over carcases beneath it. Sometimes birds of prey do their plucking up in the trees, spreading feathers over a wide area, and it is not immediately possible to link these scattered feathers with plucking.

With knowledge of the life and feeding habits and hunting methods of birds of prey, it is possible to determine with some certainty the originator of a fresh feeding site, based on its location, the size of the prey and the manner of its treatment. The

following information on some of the commonest feeding sites may help.

Among birds of prey, those most specialised for catching other birds are the *goshawk*, the *sparrowhawk* and the *falcons* excluding the kestrel, which primarily feeds on small rodents.

Sparrowhawk and goshawk feeding sites are very similar and cannot usually be distinguished with any certainty.

The prey is brought to a partially hidden spot at the forest edge or a similar place, where the plucking is often carried out on a raised platform, such as a tree stump, stone or mound.

The sparrowhawk's prey is usually small birds such as tits, sparrows and thrushes, but the female, somewhat larger than the male, can catch birds as big as pigeons and partridges. The prey is generally plucked at certain preferred spots. In the breeding season it is possible to find 50-70 (sometimes even more) plucking sites within a small area some distance from the nest, which is often found in a dense stand. At other times, too, sparrowhawks often do their plucking at certain selected spots.

The female goshawk, considerably larger and stronger than the male, can catch and carry a victim the size of a duck, while the male can only manage prey up to the size of a pigeon. In the breeding season, the goshawk uses several scattered plucking sites, but at other times, like the sparrowhawk, it will have certain preferred plucking sites.

Peregrine falcon feeding sites are mostly quite characteristic. Like the goshawk, it can catch large birds such as pigeons, gulls and ducks, but its plucking sites are always out

Osprey with its prey.

in the open. Sometimes, however, the prey is plucked up in a tree, but then always on an exposed branch high up. The peregrine falcon mostly eats the breast meat only, leaving the rest. The flight feathers are not pulled out, and the wings and breast skeleton remain connected. It is self-evident that this bird's open feeding sites, with their lavish leavings, are soon visited by crows, gulls and foxes etc.

Remains of mammals

Some birds of prey, such as *buzzards*, *harriers* and *kestrels*, feed largely on small rodents, but many other birds of prey also catch mammals, and a great number of them are carrion-eaters. When a goshawk or sparrowhawk feeds on a mammal, it often plucks the fur out, just as it would do with a bird's feathers, while the other birds of prey pull the skin off in strips.

Remains of fish

Feeding sites with fish remains can be found in areas frequented by the *osprey*.

Hare partially devoured by a buzzard. The hare was not killed by the buzzard, which is unable to kill such a large prey.

Other feeding signs

Animals looking for food in the earth often leave conspicuous holes. On page 160 there is a description of a fox's excavation of small rodents' nests; here there is no doubt what species the prey are, but often you can come across funnel-shaped holes or scrapings 10-15 cm deep, where it is not immediately obvious what the animal was hunting. These are usually places where a badger has dug or scraped for worms or insects. Meadows and lawns infested with cockchafer grubs may show signs where a badger has clawed the grass out in tufts in order to get hold of grubs feeding on the grass roots. Similar feeding signs, though considerably more severe, appear when a wild boar roots or just ploughs through the ground with its snout as it searches for insects, roots or fungi.

Bee and wasps' nests

Occasionally one finds grubbed up nests of ground-dwelling bees or wasps, with their remains spread over the soil. This is the feeding site of a badger, or perhaps a honey buzzard.

Badger: badgers are keen to get at the honey stored in bees' nests, and there are many examples of badgers knocking over and breaking open beehives to get the honey.

Honey buzzard: the honey buzzard is unusual among birds of prey, for it feeds to a large extent on insects, especially wasps and their larvae and pupae. In particular it hunts out the nests of ground-dwelling species, digging them out with its claws, and then picking out individual larvae or pupae with its beak.

Great tit: in autumn, when wasp colonies are on the wane, you can often see a great

Snout marks left by a badger hunting for earthworms. Note the worm tunnel in the centre of the picture.

Wasps' nest robbed by a badger.

Anthill torn apart by a bear.

tit, breaking apart wasps' nests that are in the open to get at the few remaining larvae and pupae.

Anthills

In winter, large holes or tunnels can be seen leading far into the wood ants' mound. These are made by green woodpeckers as they tunnel in to find pupae and adult ants that are overwintering.

Cowpats

The surfaces of older cowpats are often pierced through with large and small holes. The smaller holes are made by insects, developing into larvae within the cowpat and boring their way out through the surface when they hatch. The larger holes come from starlings, curlews or other birds, which stick their beaks into the cowpat to get at the insect larvae. Badgers also often visit

cowpats, hunting for dung beetles, either turning them round with their forepaws or breaking them apart in order to get at the beetles.

Sand and mudflats

In wet sand at the beach and on mud banks by lakes and rivers at low water, you can nearly always see large numbers of small holes, made when waders stick their beaks in the ground to hunt for crustaceans and worms. The soft ground means that the

Starlings forage on cowpats (above), which can become completely riddled with holes (below).

Holes left by the beak of an oystercatcher.

Song thrush, removing a snail from its crushed shell.

birds leave clear footprints, and these help determine the identity of the birds (see page 85).

Snail shells

On the ground around a stone, a fallen branch or on a tree stump, you can some-times find a large number of smashed, empty snail shells. This is the feeding site, often known as the 'anvil', of the *song thrush*. The bird is not able to break the shell by pecking, but, holding the shell tight in its beak, it hits it against something hard until it smashes.

The *blackbird*, unable to perform this trick, might watch the song thrush as it works, in order to rush in and snatch the snail the instant the shell is smashed.

Gulls and *crows* have another ingenious method for cracking open creatures covered by a hard shell. At low water they pick up shellfish, snails or crabs, and drop them from the air onto stones to smash them.

Rats and several *other small rodents* also eat snails, but as their feeding sites are con-cealed, rather than out in the open like those of the song thrush, they are rarely no-ticed. They often gnaw holes a little way up the shell and follow the coils down as they eat the snail. The last part of the snail is ap-parently pulled out, as the last broad coil is normally not damaged.

Antlers and bones

Antlers and bones that lie on the forest floor for a lengthy period are often gnawed by various animals – presumably for their calcium content. This is usually the work of small rodents, whose toothmarks are clearly visible as fine stripes.

Pineapple galls

On the forest floor of a sprucewood you can often find spruce twigs with pineapple galls that have been gnawed. These galls, caused by aphids, lie at the base of the previous year's shoot, and are much sought-after by squirrels. It is actually the aphids the squirrels want, and in order to get at them they bite off the shoot with the gall. After gnawing the insects out, they drop the twig to the ground.

Roe deer antler gnawed by mice.

Frog remains

In meadows and bogs and by lakes and rivers in springtime, you sometimes find some strange whitish lumps of slime, which on closer inspection prove to be the large oviducts of a frog. This phenomenon is due to an animal eating a frog but leav-

Spruce twig with pineapple gall attacked by squirrels.

Fresh frog remains. The egg masses are clearly visible.

Great grey shrike with prey impaled on a twig. This allows the shrike to tear its prey apart while keeping both feet free so it can hold on to the branch.

ing the inedible oviducts. In most cases they are the remains of a buzzard's meal, but may also be scraps or vomit from an otter or a polecat.

Impaled animals

Sometimes one finds large insects or even mice or lizards impaled on the thorns of bushes such as blackthorn and hawthorn. These are the feeding sites or food stores of shrikes. It is primarily the red-backed shrike that impales its prey in this way, but by no means all do it. Occasionally one al-

so sees barbed wire used for impaling prey. The great grey shrike, which feeds to a considerable extent on small birds, mice and suchlike as well as on large insects, does not generally impale its prey, wedging it instead in the angle of a branch or a split in the bark.

Eggshells

In spring in particular, birds' eggs can often be seen lying on the ground. In most cases these are the shells of hatched eggs, as adult birds normally remove shells from the nest

173

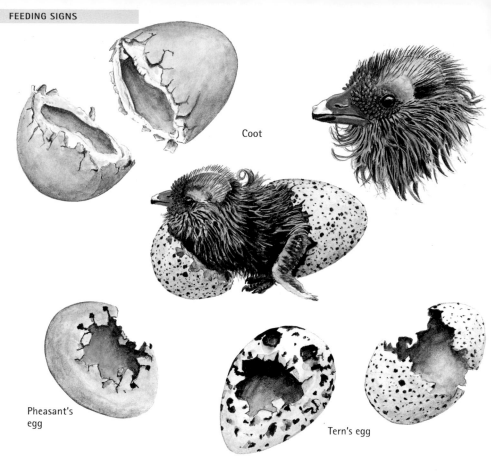

Coot

Pheasant's
egg

Tern's egg

*Top left – mallard egg. Its membrane shows that it hatched naturally. Top right –
coot chick, with its egg tooth visible on its beak.*

*Bottom left is a pheasant's egg, after attack by a predatory mammal; it shows the
marks of canine teeth (e.g. polecat or marten). Bottom right – tern's egg, marked
by a gull (centre) and a crow (right).*

by flying away with them in their beaks and
dropping them elsewhere. An exception,
however, are birds such as ducks, gamebirds
and gulls, that make their nests on the
ground, and whose young leave the nest

soon after hatching. Their eggshells are often seen left crushed in the nest.

However, eggs are much sought after by
a number of animals, and some of the shells
one finds are scraps from an animal's meal.

In most cases it is not difficult to determine whether a shell comes from a hatched egg or whether its contents have been eaten by an animal. It is often also possible to determine what kind of animal the egg-thief was from the way in which the egg was treated.

At the point of hatching, most bird embryos have an 'egg tooth', a hard, horny point near the tip of the upper mandible. This is used to cut or break a crack in the shell right round the egg nearest to the blunt end. As the crack is worked on, small bits of shell break off, meaning that when the egg finally breaks into two fairly regular sections, the strong membrane covering the inside will protrude slightly from the edge. As it dries, this will gradually curl inwards. Inside the shell there is no trace of yolk or white. The two shell sections are often found together, as the bird fits the smaller section in the larger for transporting the shell away from the nest, so that it only needs to make one journey.

When an egg is pecked or bitten open by another animal, the shell membrane will *not* protrude, and the curl along the shell edge described above will not be there. Instead, you can nearly always see clear remnants of the yellow yolk and a shining layer of egg white on the inside of the shell. If the egg was close to hatching, there will also often be signs of blood.

The various members of the *crow* family are amongst our worst egg-thieves, robbing nests in trees as well as on the ground. They pick up the egg in their beak and carry it to an open place, a woodland path or a field, where they put it on the ground and peck an irregular hole in its side.

Gulls are also egg-eaters, but are only

Hen's egg, eaten by a polecat. Two holes, made by the canines, are clearly visible.

able to get eggs from nests on the ground. They do not usually remove the eggs, but peck holes in them while they are still in the nest, or at most, roll them a little way away. It is interesting to observe how ducks, for example, which often nest near gull colonies, always cover their eggs with down or other nest materials when they leave the nest, so that gulls and crows do not spot them. If you chase a bird from its nest, you must always make sure that you cover the eggs up in the same way, otherwise the nest will certainly be robbed.

Many garden-owners have had the bitter experience of having nest boxes robbed by the *great spotted woodpecker* pecking holes in them. However, it is not the eggs the woodpeckers are after but the newly-hatched

175

young, which they can hear moving about and chirping inside the box. These attacks can be prevented by covering the boxes with a relatively hard metal sheet; woodpeckers can peck through a lead sheet, however, with no difficulty.

Several mammals steal eggs. The most habitual egg-eaters are the martens, as many poultry farmers have found. The eggs are generally removed from the nest, the animal taking one at a time and carrying it away in its mouth to eat in a quiet spot. The *pine marten* and the *fox* often bury eggs under moss or a similar place for later use. Martens get eggs open in a rather distinctive way, biting across the egg, making an elongated, almost square hole, through which they lick up the egg contents. The hedgehog is also very fond of eggs, and near colonies of birds such as gulls, it will feed mostly on eggs and newly-hatched young birds during the breeding season. It bites an irregular hole on the side of the egg and laps up the contents. The fox generally bites the egg, crushing the whole shell, and licking up the white and the yolk.

DROPPINGS

Actual size

Bat p. 183

Hedgehog p. 182

Beaver p. 185

Hare p. 183

Rabbit p. 184

Squirrel p. 184

Coypu p. 186

Voles

Mice

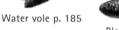

Muskrat p. 185

Brown rat p. 186

Water vole p. 185

Black rat p. 186

Norway lemming p. 185

House mouse p. 186

Field vole p. 185

Wood mouse p. 186

Badger p. 188

Beech marten p. 189

Fox p. 187

Polecat p. 190

Weasel p. 191

178

Actual size

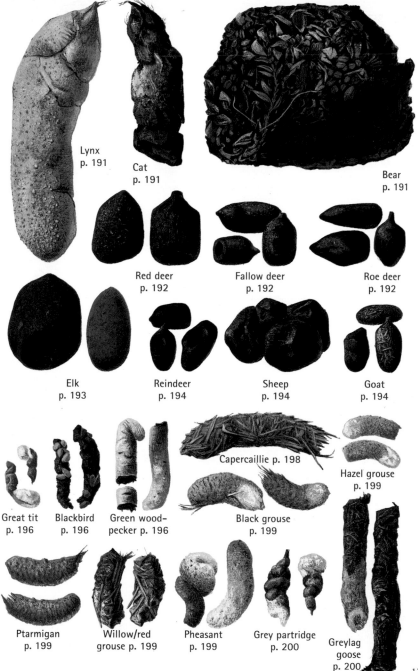

Lynx
p. 191

Cat
p. 191

Bear
p. 191

Red deer
p. 192

Fallow deer
p. 192

Roe deer
p. 192

Elk
p. 193

Reindeer
p. 194

Sheep
p. 194

Goat
p. 194

Great tit
p. 196

Blackbird
p. 196

Green wood-
pecker p. 196

Capercaillie p. 198

Black grouse
p. 199

Hazel grouse
p. 199

Ptarmigan
p. 199

Willow/red
grouse p. 199

Pheasant
p. 199

Grey partridge
p. 200

Greylag
goose
p. 200

Animal droppings are important signs, found everywhere in natural surroundings. Many people may think that this is an unsavoury subject, but droppings provide a great deal of interesting information, not just on the animals' eating habits, but also on other aspects of their life and behaviour.

Droppings consist of the indigestible parts of food, such as fur, feathers, splinters of bone, pieces of chitin from insects, plant matter with more or less empty cells, mucous, cells from the intestinal tract, along with large quantities of living and dead bacteria. Fresh mammal droppings in particular have a scent so strong that even humans can perceive it. This scent is extremely important for animals, for not only every species, but also every individual, has its own particular scent.

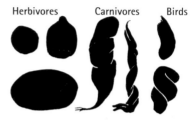

Droppings of domestic goat.

Examples of shapes of droppings.

Mammal droppings

Some mammals have special scent glands just inside the anus, which transfer a secretion to the droppings as they are discharged. These glands are only fully developed in sexually mature animals, and are most active in the mating season. The scent indicates to other members of the species that the animal is sexually receptive – information that is obviously very important for ensuring that the sexes can find each other. In some cases animals use droppings to scent-mark their territory (see also page 244); this applies to the fox and the rabbit, for example (see pages 245 and 184).

Rabbits, and also some rodents and shrews, produce two types of dropping; as well as the usual droppings we find in the wild, they also discharge soft, dark and slimy droppings, which the animals eat again immediately after they have been discharged. The reason for this is not entirely clear, but it is thought to be connected with making use of the large amount of B-vitamins in the gut, formed by bacteria in the intestinal tract.

Closer examination of the droppings can provide a great deal of information on what the animal has eaten. Pieces of chitin can identify which insects it has eaten, and the cell structure of plant remains can often indicate which plant species the animals have been concentrating on. The presence of bones, feathers and fur in predators' drop-

pings likewise shows which animals they have eaten, but it is important to bear in mind that just because a predator has eaten an animal, it is far from certain that it also killed it. Most predators are in fact keen carrion-eaters, which partially explains why it is relatively rare for us to come across dead animals in the wild. Of course, it is only possible for specialists to make accurate identifications of what an animal has eaten. In most cases, though, it is easy for anyone to determine whether a dropping comes from a herbivore or a carnivore, and the keen naturalist may be able to make an even closer identification.

The amount of droppings discharged by an animal depends on the type of food and on how well the animal can use it. A plant diet is poor in easily accessible nutrients, and herbivores therefore need to eat large amounts; they also subsequently produce large quantities of droppings, which always clearly reveal their presence. Meat, on the other hand, has a high nutritional value, which is easily accessible, and of which nearly all can be used by carnivores; so their droppings are sparser.

In terms of shape and size, droppings are generally characteristic for each mammal species, though the size will depend to some extent on the animal's age, with the droppings of young animals being naturally smaller than those of adults. The composition of the food also affects the shape. Juicy grass will make soft, sometimes deliquescent droppings, while hay makes dry, hard ones. In some cases it is possible to make a clear distinction between an animal's summer and winter droppings.

Colour can also provide information on what the animal has eaten. Young animals still being suckled have light grey-brown droppings, and animals that have eaten strongly-coloured berries, such as bilberries, will leave droppings clearly coloured by them.

The droppings of herbivores are often small and round, while those of carnivores are usually cylindrical or sausage-shaped and pointed at one end.

When identifying mammal droppings it is important to note their position, as well as shape, size, content, colour and smell. Many animals let their droppings fall at random, while others use special latrines, where large quantities may eventually collect. Some animals, such as the badger and the domestic cat, dig a small hole in the ground to deposit their droppings, after which the cat – though not the badger – carefully covers the hole again. As described earlier, some animals, e.g. fox, use their droppings to scent-mark their territory; in such cases, the droppings are often left high up, on a tree stump, a stone or a tussock, so that the scent can spread widely.

The following pages describe the droppings most frequently spotted in the wild. They are in a systematic order, as in previous sections (see page 10).

Hedgehog

Hedgehog droppings are cylindrical, normally shiny black, and generally pointed at one end. There is a great variation in size, but the average is 8-10 mm thick and 3-4 cm long. They are mainly composed of insect remains, their chitin parts clearly visible on the surface, making them shine. Sometimes they also contain fur, feathers and small pieces of bone. At the end of summer and in autumn they often contain berry remains. If the hedgehog has eaten a mouse or a bird, its droppings will be dull, twisted and rather thin, and may be confused with the droppings of one of the smaller marten species.

The hedgehog deposits its droppings when foraging at night, and they can be found randomly spread on lawns etc. (see page 178).

Shrew

These droppings are very small, 2-4 mm long and 1-2 mm thick. They are generally

Hedgehog droppings, in June.

dark brown or black, and are often pointed at the ends. They are composed largely of insect remains, and can be found under pieces of wood, stones etc.

Bat

Bat droppings can somewhat resemble mouse droppings, but can be distinguished by the fact that they are far more porous, and that they consist exclusively of finely divided insect remains. The colour is dark-brown to black, and the size varies from species to species. The serotine, one of Europe's largest bats, has droppings that are usually 6-8 mm long and 3 mm thick (see page 178).

The droppings are often found in large quantities at the bats' sleeping places in lofts or cellars, in hollow trees or caves. Several species also like to live in bird nesting-boxes.

Bat droppings on roof timbers. Often the only visible trace of the presence of bats.

Hare

Hare droppings are easy to recognise. In winter they are light brown or yellow-brown, slightly flattened, but otherwise regularly round and firm, with a diameter of 15-20 mm. They are composed of rather coarse plant matter, clearly distinguishable on the surface. The colour varies according to what the hare has eaten, and becomes progressively lighter on exposure to rain and sun. In the summer, when the hare feeds on juicier food than in the winter, the droppings are darker, sometimes almost black. They have a softer consistency than the winter ones, and can sometimes be slightly pointed (see page 178 and photo on next page).

The droppings appear mostly at the hare's feeding sites, where they often lie in small heaps, but the hare also characteristically empties its gut shortly before seeking out its day-lair or form, and within a short distance you can often see droppings scattered singly in the prints or along the hare's run.

Mountain hare

The droppings of the mountain hare are so similar to those of the hare that it is impossible to distinguish between them with any certainty.

Rabbit

Rabbit droppings are very similar to those of the hare, but are smaller, approx. 10 mm in diameter, and more spherical (see

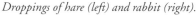

Droppings of hare (left) and rabbit (right).

page 178). In contrast to hares, rabbits tend to deposit their droppings on raised places, tussocks, and molehills etc., where they establish special latrines, often with large, very conspicuous amounts of droppings. This is linked to the fact that rabbits often use droppings to scent-mark their territory (see page 244), and on the edges of a warren it is often possible to see latrines positioned on tracks, often close to places where they cross. When a strange rabbit comes into the area it will tread on these dropping-heaps and their scent will warn it that this area is occupied. Since these latrine-spots are generally used for long periods, the extra fertilisation of the ground has a marked effect on the local vegetation.

Squirrel

Squirrel droppings are short and almost spherical, often slightly flattened at one end and with a small point at the other. In summer they are brown, 5-8 mm long and 5-6 mm thick; in winter they are dark brown or black and somewhat smaller. They contain finely-divided plant matter, distinguishable on the surface, but insect parts are also found in them (see page 178).

It is very rare to find their droppings in summer, but in winter they can be seen in the snow, either directly, or indirectly through the small holes created when they fell. If they lie on the snow for a while it will turn yellow-brown, making them easier to spot.

Beaver

Beaver droppings are short and thick, often almost spherical and with the hint of a point at one end. They are approx. 2 cm thick, 2-4 cm long and dark brown in colour. In consistency they greatly resemble hare droppings, being composed principally of rather coarse plant matter, clearly visible on the surface (see page 178).

The beaver always deposits its droppings in the water, but they can sometimes be seen floating close to the banks.

Vole

The many species of the vole family have rather uniform, cylindrical droppings, generally rounded at the ends. In summer, when voles feed mostly on green plants, they are usually greenish in colour, while they are brownish in winter, when the voles eat bark, roots and the like (see page 178).

Apart from particular species such as the muskrat and the water vole (see below), whose droppings can be recognised by their size, it is impossible to distinguish the droppings of the various voles. For identification it is therefore necessary to rely on other signs such as feeding signs, as well as on the location of the find and your own knowledge of which species are found in that locality.

Muskrat droppings are approx. 12-14 mm long and 5 mm thick. They are found near streams and lakes, where they are deposited very conspicuously in spring on stones and suchlike (territorial marking); later in the year they are mainly discharged in the water (see page 178).

Water vole droppings are 7-10 mm long and 3-4 mm thick.

Droppings of Norway lemming.

Field vole droppings are only 6-7 mm long and 2-3 mm thick; they are found in small heaps at the vole's feeding sites (see page 178).

Norway lemming droppings resemble those of the field vole. They are commonly seen on heaths, occurring in heaps that can be extremely large in 'lemming years', when lemmings appear in large numbers (see page 178).

Muskrat.

Droppings of a member of the mouse family: brown rat.

Mouse

This is a family of numerous species, with droppings less uniform and regular than those of voles (see page 178).

Brown rat droppings are cylindrical, generally have blunt ends and are approx. 17 mm long and 6 mm thick, though the size varies greatly. This rat tends to have special latrines, but droppings are often found in random places, frequently a small number together (see page 178).

Black rat (**house rat, roof rat**) droppings are shorter and thinner than those of the brown rat, approx. 10 mm long and 2-3 mm thick,

and arc often slightly curved and pointed at the ends (see page 178). If you have rats in your loft, you can easily tell the black rat from the brown by the location of the droppings: the black rat drops them all over the loft, while the brown rat leaves them in corners or along the walls. In Britain the black rat is rare and local.

House mouse droppings are small and cylindrical, usually approx. 6 mm long and 2-2.5 mm thick.

Wood mouse and yellow-necked mouse droppings are short and thick in comparison with those of the house mouse (see page 178).

Coypu droppings are 2-3 cm long and a little under 1 cm wide, with a characteristic finely-furrowed surface. They occur near streams and in marshy areas (see page 178).

Carnivores

Carnivore droppings are generally cylindrical, and usually pointed at one end. Some animals, however, including the badger and the otter, often have soft or runny droppings. The colour is usually dark brown, but can vary according to the food eaten. Many carnivores are keen berry eaters, and if the berries are strongly coloured, like bilberries, this will affect the colour of the droppings.

Sometimes the surface of the droppings may have a brittle, white coating, which may also form part of the droppings themselves. This is an excretion of phosphates, originating in bone fragments dissolved in the animal's digestive tract. This can, for example, be observed in dogs that have had many bones.

The most conspicuous elements of the

Fox droppings. The white colour is due to the large number of bones in the fox's diet. Fox droppings are often found slightly above ground level – see photo on page 244 – where they function as territorial markers.

The droppings of the dog (top) and the domestic cat are certainly associated with the homes of humans, but they are often also found out in the wild and may be confused with the droppings of wild animals.

droppings are fur, feathers, teeth and bone fragments, and in summer, insect remains, berries and other fruit. Based on these remains, it is often possible to determine precisely what the animal has eaten. Fresh droppings of carnivores always have a sharp, acrid 'carnivore smell', which is particularly strong in the mating season, and many animals also use their droppings to scent-mark their territories.

Fox droppings are sausage-shaped, usually 8-10 cm long and approx. 2 cm thick, spirally twisted, and pointed at one end. Sometimes they drop in small sections, and then only the last section is pointed. The colour varies from black to grey, but in autumn, when the fox eats a lot of berries, the droppings often take on their colour. They are composed of fur, feathers and bone fragments from small rodents and birds, in summer often also containing pieces of chitin from insects, particularly beetles' elytra, and remains of various berries and other fruit. The fox uses its strong-smelling droppings to mark its territory, so they are often deposited above ground level, e.g. on a tree stump, stone or tussock, from which the scent can spread easily. They may, however, be left on paths or on the animal's tracks (see page 178).

187

Wolf droppings in snow, with a large fur content.

Badger droppings deposited in a small hollow the badger has scraped in the ground.

Wolf droppings resemble large dog droppings. They are dark grey, 10-15 cm long and 2.5-3 cm thick, and, like the fox's, are deposited in high spots in the terrain; they are often made more conspicuous by the wolf having scraped the earth with its rear paws, as dogs do.

Badger droppings may be dry and sausage-shaped, or soft and runny, depending on what the badger has eaten. The sausage-shaped droppings resemble those of the fox, but are more cylindrical, with a rough, uneven surface. They are composed largely of insect remains, fur from small rodents, seeds and berries (see page 178). However, the most characteristic feature is their positioning. The badger has special latrines, where the droppings are deposited in small, oblong holes about 10 cm deep, scraped in the earth by the badger using its front paws.

The holes are not covered after use, and may be used several times. They are often found near the sett or in particular areas right next to a track. They can be more isolated, but are nearly always by a well-used track.

Otter droppings are tarry, black and slimy when fresh, with a characteristic, long-lasting oily smell. As time passes they become light grey and crumbly. They are generally composed of fish scales and bones, and pieces of shell from crustaceans etc.

The droppings are most frequently found – often in small amounts – in raised sites along the banks of rivers, on a stone or tree stump on the bank, for example. They are often also deposited where a ditch empties into a larger water system, and sometimes placed on a platform of grass or sand scraped together by the otter itself, in the middle of a bare bank. This characteristic positioning shows that the otter uses its droppings as scent markers to guide other members of its species.

Pine marten and beech marten: the droppings of these two animals cannot be distinguished by appearance, but may be identified by their smell and position (see below). They are usually 8-10 cm long and 1.2 cm thick, sausage-shaped, generally twisted and pointed. They are composed of fur, feathers, bone splinters; also, in late

Otter droppings (spraint), placed high up in dry vegetation, so it can function as a territorial marker.

Marten droppings. Left, pine marten. Right, beech marten.

Mink droppings.

summer and autumn, berry remains and plum and cherry stones. They are dark grey or black in colour (see page 178).

The *pine marten's* droppings have a pronounced and quite agreeable musky smell. They are often found deposited on raised places such as stones, tree stumps, woodpiles or fallen tree trunks. The *beech marten's* droppings are foul-smelling, and in lofts or out-houses it can often be seen to establish special latrines on boxes or similar places, where there may be large quantities of droppings.

Polecat and mink: the droppings of these two animals greatly resemble each other. When firm, they take the usual marten shape, i.e. sausage-shaped, twisted and pointed, and are usually 6-8 cm long and approx. 9 mm thick, so slightly smaller than those of pine and beech martens'. They are generally composed of fur, feathers and bone fragments, as well as berry remains. If the animals have eaten fish and amphibians, the droppings are loose and deliquescent. The polecat's droppings in particular have a very sour and unpleasant smell, but despite this, they are not used for scent marking, and are inconspicuously placed. The polecat often has a special latrine at its home (see page 178).

Stoat droppings resemble the dry droppings of the polecat, but are smaller, approx. 5 mm thick. They contain fur, feathers and bone remains from small rodents. They are often placed above ground level.

Weasel droppings are like those of the stoat, but even smaller, approx. 2 mm thick (see page 178).

Cat (domestic cat) droppings are sausage-shaped, usually 6-8 cm long and 1-1.5 cm thick, though they can also be somewhat runny. They are deposited in a small hollow, which the cat scrapes in the earth or snow with its forepaws. After use the hole is carefully covered. Urine, which is strong-smelling like the droppings, is dealt with in the same way. It has been observed that the wild cat only hides its droppings and urine in this way within its own territory. On the edges of its territory, droppings are conspicuously deposited on tree stumps, stones and similar places, like fox droppings. Here the strong-smelling droppings are used to warn other wild cats of the territory limits (see page 179).

Lynx droppings resemble those of the cat, but are much larger. They contain feathers, fur and bone remains. Like the cat, the lynx carefully covers its droppings with earth or snow (see page 179).

Bear droppings are cylindrical in summer and can reach the thickness of a human wrist. They are deposited in large heaps, and are composed of fur, bone fragments, and remains of various insects and plants. In autumn, when the bear eats various berries, its droppings are runny (see page 179).

Wild boar

Wild boar droppings are normally sausage-shaped, approx. 7 cm thick, consisting of elongated balls, stuck or more or less fused together.

Bear droppings.

Red deer droppings.

Fallow deer droppings.

Deer

Deer droppings are bean-like – short, cylindrical or almost spherical, and often have a little point. They have a smooth surface and, when fresh, are usually black and covered with a thin shiny layer of slime; this, however, dries fast. Externally they reveal nothing of their contents, and it is only when broken open that the yellow-brown or greenish colour of finely-divided plant remains is visible. In summer, the droppings are soft and sticky, and often more or less joined together. Deer dropings are generally found in quite large mounds at the feeding sites, but can also be seen randomly deposited.

Red deer: the adult deer's droppings are 20-25 mm long and 13-18 mm thick. When fresh they are black and shiny, gradually becoming a dull dark brown. In shape they are cylindrical and frequently pointed at one end, while the other end is either rounded or has a faint hollow. The male's droppings are larger than those of the female and are chiefly of the type that has the faint hollow at one end, while those of the female are usually rounded. Summer droppings are often quite soft and lumped together (see page 179).

Fallow deer droppings resemble those of red deer, but are smaller, generally 10-15 mm long and 8-12 mm wide. The winter droppings consist of individual pellets, whereas the summer droppings are joined-together lumps (see page 179).

Roe deer droppings are 10-14 mm long and 7-10 mm wide, and are black or dark brown. Winter droppings are short, cylindrical, sometimes almost spherical, often rounded at one end and pointed at the

Roe deer droppings, October.

other. In summer, the droppings are often deposited in large, connected lumps, with a furrowed surface. The droppings occur in mounds at the deer's feeding sites, but it is also common for the deer to discharge droppings while walking, so they can be seen individually scattered between the deer's hoofprints over quite long stretches.

Roe deer droppings are very similar to those of sheep and goats (see page 179).

Elk droppings are easily recognisable by their colour and size. They are yellow-brown or black-brown, according to their food. Winter droppings are dry, light and firm (see photo below), while the summer droppings are darker, soft, and damp, with a tendency to lump together. Winter droppings from adult deer are 20-30 mm long and 15-20 mm wide. There are two main kinds: they are either almost *spherical*, often with a faint point at one end and somewhat flattened at the other, perhaps with a faint hollow, or they are more *elongated with rounded ends*, perhaps slightly pointed at one end. Between these two main kinds, however, there is a large variety of shapes. It is not, as was once thought, the bulls which deposit the round ones and the cows which deposit the elongated ones. It is not possible to distinguish between the two sexes' droppings (see page 179).

Reindeer: winter droppings are 12-15 mm long and 7-10 mm thick; their colour is very dark – black or brown-black. Summer

Elk – winter droppings.

Elk – summer droppings.

Mouflon droppings.

Droppings of domestic sheep.

droppings are yellow-brown, soft and often runny (see page 179).

Sheep, goats and relatives

Mouflon droppings are composed of balls a centimetre in diameter, which are discharged compressed into sausages or lumps, so they often lose their shape and become angular, sometimes pyramidal.

Domestic sheep droppings resemble those of the mouflon (see page 179).

Goat droppings are bean-shaped – cylindrical, approx. 1cm long, sometimes slightly flat at one or both ends. They are often found in small heaps (see page 179 and photo on page 182).

Chamois droppings are almost spherical, approx. 1.5 cm in diameter. They are often discharged in a compressed shape, so the individual droppings become somewhat flattened.

Musk ox: winter droppings are similar to those the reindeer, but are larger (2 cm

long and 1 cm wide) and oval in shape. In summer, moist food makes their droppings runny.

Cow droppings are normally a brown, viscous, circular mass. When dried, the 'cow-pat' is flat and cake-like in shape, with undigested plant matter clearly visible.

Soft summer droppings of musk ox.

194

Bird droppings

While waste from the gut (droppings) and the waste that is excreted via the kidneys (urine), are released separately in mammals, in birds they are discharged more or less together through the cloaca. Birds' urine is usually whitish and viscous, strongly affecting the droppings, often making them highly conspicuous.

Many birds, such as birds of prey, owls, crows and gulls, get rid of most of the indigestible elements of their food by coughing them up as pellets (see page 205). These species will not normally have identifiable food remains in their droppings, though information on its composition can naturally be gained from their pellets. By examining the droppings of birds that do not produce pellets, however, it is often possible to form an idea of what they have eaten. The numerous insectivores, including the green woodpecker (see page 179) will have remains of insects' indigestible chitin in their droppings, and the droppings of birds that have eaten berries will contain seeds that have passed unscathed through the digestive tract. This plays a large part in the seed dispersal of many plants, for birds often discharge the seeds far away from the place where they were eaten. When berries are strongly coloured, e.g. bilberries and elderberries, the colour very much affects the droppings, and this helps to reveal what the birds have eaten. In pronounced herbivores, such as swans and geese, many ducks and gamebirds, fresh droppings are often greenish and relatively firm, and on the surface it is often possible to clearly spot the plant matter content.

In terms of shape and consistency, bird droppings can roughly be divided into three

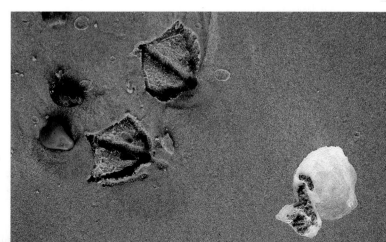

Gulls' droppings may be found almost anywhere, but it is not always possible to confirm that they really do come from a gull. Here the footprints help make the identification more certain.

main types: watery, roundish semi-firm, and cylindrical firm droppings. There are, however, many intermediate forms, and the droppings of an individual species can vary a great deal in appearance, depending on its food. In reality, it is relatively rare to be able to identify with certainty the species of bird from its droppings alone. It is therefore only really possible to give a general description of the various commonly-occurring types of droppings.

Watery droppings

The droppings of *birds of prey* are of the watery type, discharged in a whitish stream, as the birds lift their tails in the air to spray droppings and urine backwards. There are droppings at the birds' feeding sites (see pages 166-167) and resting places, but most droppings are seen around the nest, where the young spray them over the edge of the

nest, creating white spots on the branches and the underlying ground.

Herons and *cormorants* have similar droppings, and as these birds raise many young together in colonies, the nesting tree and the ground beneath will be completely covered with droppings and urine. Since these products are strongly corrosive, the vegetation cannot survive this splattering in the long term, and, particularly in cormorant colonies, the nesting tree and the ground vegetation beneath the colony dies relatively quickly.

Firm droppings

The droppings and white urine of *passerine* young are covered with a slimy membrane; they form a quite firm, almost spherical lump (faecal sac). It is discharged immediately after the young bird has been fed, and the adult bird, waiting at the edge of the

The droppings of birds of prey are watery, as can be clearly seen in this picture of a goshawk.

On the forest floor the droppings of birds of prey can be seen as a thin coating on leaves etc. This is from a buzzard.

△ *Cormorant droppings are often spotted on stones or nesting trees.*

Droppings on the ground or against a wall, as here, betray the presence of a swallows' nest. ▽

nest for a moment, takes the lump in its beak and flies away with it. This is easily observed in nest-boxes: you see an adult bird with food in its beak flying into the box, only to leave it again a moment later carrying a lump of excrement. Removing the droppings keeps the nest and the young birds' down clean. Once the young have reached a certain size, the parent birds no longer wait for the droppings; they are discharged at the edge of the nest, to be later removed by the adults or eventually just pushed over the edge to fall to the ground below.

The droppings of the adult bird lack the membrane described above, and are there-

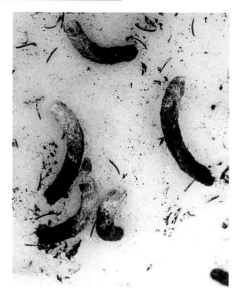

Winter droppings of capercaillie.

Droppings of black grouse.

fore runnier. Their droppings generally consist of a semi-firm, elongated lump of excrement surrounded by whitish, slimy urine that is more or less runny.

Gamebirds

The droppings of gamebirds are faintly curved, cylindrical and, particularly in winter, dry and firm. They are usually composed of plant fragments, which can clearly be distinguished on the surface. The colour varies, but is generally yellow-brown to dark-brown, and there is often a whitish coating of urine at one end. In summer, and particularly in the berry season, the droppings are softer and lumpier. They are found singly at the birds' feeding sites or in heaps on or under their resting places. The capercaillie, for example, produces firm, cylindrical droppings, which are then coated with a soft, brownish substance produced by the caecum.

As the droppings of gamebirds are firm and quite long-lasting, particularly in winter, it is often possible to identify the species by size and content.

Capercaillie droppings are very large, as long as a human little finger and approx. 1.2 cm thick. The male's are larger than those of the female. In winter they are composed almost entirely of pine needle remains, clearly seen on the surface of the droppings. When fresh they are green-yellow, but gradually become brownish or greyish (see page 179).

Black grouse droppings are about half the size of those of the capercaillie, and more compact. In winter they are pale yellow when fresh, gradually becoming brown-grey. They are usually composed of birch

Hazel grouse droppings.

Ptarmigan droppings.

bud remains, with their dark scales clearly distinguishable amongst the fine-grained mass (see page 179).

Hazel grouse droppings are 1.5-2 cm long and 6-7 mm wide. In winter they are compact and are largely composed of catkin remains from alder, birch and hazel (see page 179).

Willow grouse and ptarmigan droppings are of a similar size to those of the hazel grouse. In winter they are frequently quite compact and fine-grained, composed of various bud remains, though they may also contain coarser plant matter, resembling the droppings of the capercaillie in consistency (see page 179).

Pheasant droppings are approx. 2 cm long and 4-5 cm thick. They generally have a

Brent goose droppings.

white lump of urine at one end. The colour varies according to the bird's food, but is usually brown-black or greenish. In winter they are generally firm, often curved or

bowed; in summer they may be runnier (see page 179).

Grey partridge and red-legged partridge droppings greatly resemble those of the pheasant, but are only half the size (see page 179).

Ruff droppings can be seen on the birds' lekking grounds on salt marshes (see page 248). However, the dancing of the males tends to smear them into large white patches.

Swans and geese

These birds being definite herbivores, their droppings are generally firm and cylindrical. They can be found in considerable numbers on salt marshes and lakeshores, and goose droppings can be seen in fields where they have been foraging.

The droppings of *geese* are composed of compressed plant fragments, and are 5-8 cm long and 10-12 mm thick. When fresh they are greenish, but gradually turn grey-brown or grey-black (see page 179).

Swan droppings resemble those of geese, but are approximately twice as large.

URINE

A fox has urinated to mark its territory.

The whitish urine of birds, discharged together with droppings and therefore described in that section, is frequently a highly conspicuous sign. The same is not the case for mammals; their urine is discharged separately from droppings, and is generally a clear fluid, varying from almost colourless to dark yellow.

In summer it can rarely be seen that an

The position of urine in relation to tracks in foxes and roe deer. See also photograph opposite.

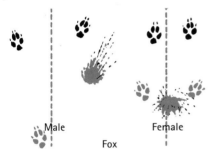

Male   Female

Fox

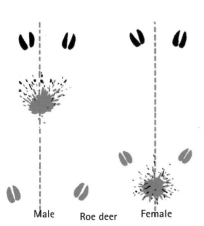

Male   Roe deer   Female

Spots of polecat urine may be seen here in the middle of its jumping tracks along a concrete wall.

animal has urinated, but it may be detected if the urine has a strong enough scent for a human to perceive it. If you walk through terrain where there are foxes, you will often notice, quite suddenly, a sour foxy smell, which almost always comes from strong-smelling fox urine. You come across it so frequently because the fox uses urine as a scent-marker, both to demonstrate to other foxes the borders of its territory, and to announce itself to the opposite sex in the mating season, when the urine has a special scent (see also page 244). The same behaviour can be observed in male dogs, which rarely empty their bladders all at once, but deposit small amounts of urine in particularly favoured spots.

In winter there are, of course, good opportunities to spot yellow urine in snow, and then you can use the footprints to identify the species that produced the urine, and sometimes even to see which sex the animal was. When a male fox urinates, it raises one hind leg like a male dog, sending a stream of urine obliquely forwards, generally beyond the three clearly-marked footprints. A female fox, however, squats down, so the urine goes between the two rear paw prints. It is also possible to identify the sex of deer from the position of urine in relation to their tracks. When deer urinate, they adopt a characteristic position with straddled rear legs, at the same time lowering themselves slightly on their rear legs. Due to the anatomical differences between the sexes, the male's urine goes between the front and rear hoof prints, while the female's goes between the rear hoof prints or slightly behind them.

PELLETS

GULLS

Black-headed gull p. 215
Fish bones

Berry remains

Beetles

Plant remains

Common gull p. 215
Fish bones

Cherry stones

Beetles

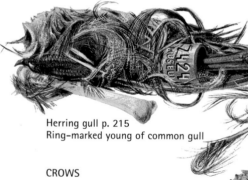

Herring gull p. 215
Ring-marked young of common gull

Mussel shells

CROWS

Crow p. 213
Small rodents

Rook p. 213
Plant remains

WADERS

Jackdaw p. 214
Plant remains, small stones

Magpie p. 214
Small rodents

Oystercatcher
Grains of sand

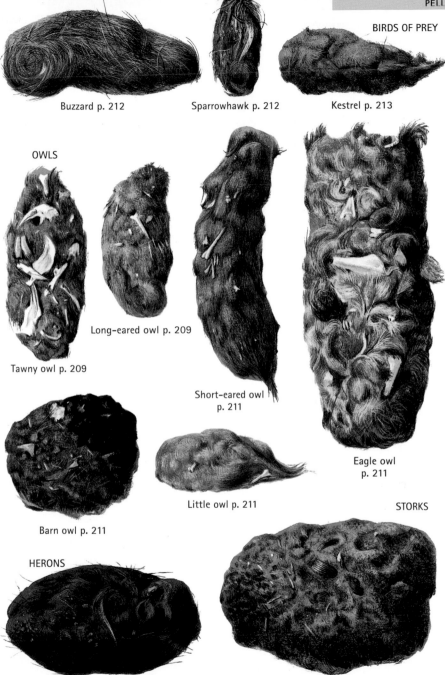

BIRDS OF PREY

Buzzard p. 212

Sparrowhawk p. 212

Kestrel p. 213

OWLS

Long-eared owl p. 209

Tawny owl p. 209

Short-eared owl
p. 211

Eagle owl
p. 211

Little owl p. 211

STORKS

Barn owl p. 211

HERONS

Grey heron p. 216

White stork p. 216

207

Cormorant pellet.

the gizzard, where it is compacted into a ball, which is then coughed up when it reaches a suitable size. Fresh pellets are covered with mucus, which eases the ball's passage through the gullet and helps keep the ball together.

On its way through the gullet, the pellet acquires its final form. The diameter of the gullet thus determines the thickness of the pellet, and since a large bird normally has a larger gullet than a smaller bird, the diameter of the pellet is an important feature in species identification. The shape of the pellet also varies to some extent from species to species; some birds, for example, produce almost spherical pellets, while those of others are cylindrical, with one or both ends rounded or pointed. The consistency depends on what the bird has eaten, and may be quite firm or so loose that the pellet easily falls apart.

Many birds get rid of any food that they cannot use by coughing it up in more or less compact balls. These consist of fur, feathers, chitin from insects, bones, pieces of shell, assorted plant matter and so on, that cannot be dissolved – or only with difficulty – by the digestive juices in the stomach. It is well known that owls produce pellets, but birds of prey, crows, gulls and many other birds also do so. For these birds, coughing up pellets is a natural phenomenon which should not be confused with the vomiting that occasionally occurs in animals that have eaten something that irritates the mucous membranes of the stomach, and react by ejecting the stomach contents through the gullet.

Birds' stomachs are divided into two generally quite sharply separated sections, the glandular stomach and the gizzard. In birds that produce pellets, the indigestible or hard-to-digest food eventually gathers in

Examining the food remnants within a pellet can provide a great deal of interesting information on what the bird has eaten. As individual species also prefer particular types of food, the content can often greatly aid identification. Finally, the individual species prefer particular habitats, so it is also important to take note of the characteristics of the spot where it was found: whether it was a field, for example, or a beach or a wood (and whether it was deciduous or coniferous) etc.

Pellets are mostly found at the resting places and nests of birds, but can also be seen at their feeding spots (see page 166). A bird normally produces around two pellets a day, and it generally coughs one up just before flying off to hunt.

Owls

It is great fun to pull owl pellets apart to see what is in them. Once you have done it the first time, it is very hard to walk past a pellet without picking it up and breaking it open to see what you can find.

Owl pellets are generally grey when dry, and characteristically always contain well-preserved bones from their prey. The skull is usually crushed, however, for owls normally kill their prey with a powerful bite to the back of the head. The bones may likewise be bitten or broken, but the digestive juices will have had virtually no effect, so even the most delicate small bones can be retrieved.

Owls generally swallow small mammals and birds whole. This, together with the fact that the digestive juices do not affect bones, means that close examination of a pellet can reveal fairly precise information on what the bird has eaten. Examinations of this kind can also be used to gain information on such things as the abundance of small rodents in a particular area.

As well as bones, the pellets contain large quantities of fur, bits of feathers, and often chitin from the exoskeleton of insects – the elytra of beetles are particularly conspicuous. Birds' gizzards are often seen as a little sac – this is the gizzard's horny material. The horny coverings from the prey's beak and claws, however, have nearly always disappeared.

The pellets of different bird species can generally be distinguished by size, shape and content – at least if this information is taken together with the spot where they were found. The following section describes the characteristics of the most frequently found pellets.

Tawny owl

A tawny owl pellet is grey, cylindrical, usually 4-6 cm long, 2-3 cm thick and somewhat pointed at one or both ends. It is often faintly curved and generally has a rather irregular surface. The contents normally consist of the remains of mice and small birds, and in some cases shrews and bits of insects. In the breeding season, when the tawny owl catches a number of medium-sized birds such as thrushes and pigeons, bones of these may also be found (see page 207). Most frequently found in dense coniferous woodland, but may also be found in churches, barns and similar places, or below favourite trees in parks and large gardens.

Pellet of long-eared owl.

209

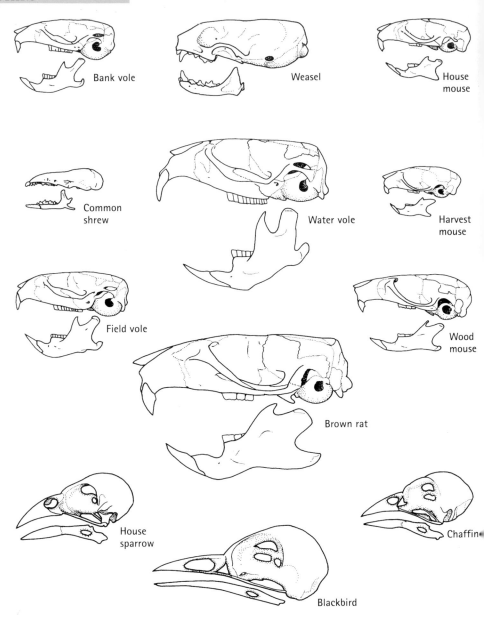

Bank vole

Weasel

House mouse

Common shrew

Water vole

Harvest mouse

Field vole

Wood mouse

Brown rat

House sparrow

Chaffinc

Blackbird

Examples of skulls found in owl pellets. Roughly life size.

Pellet of eagle owl.

Pellet of short-eared owl.

Long-eared owl

The pellet of the long-eared owl is light or dark grey, cylindrical, 4-7.5 cm long, 2-3 cm thick and rounded at one or both ends. It is thinner than that of the tawny owl, and has an even surface. Its content resembles that of the tawny owl. Frequently found in dense coniferous woodland, where in winter many can be found in spots where the owls spend the day in small groups (see page 207).

Short-eared owl

Pellet resembles that of the long-eared owl, but can be somewhat longer, and its content consists almost exclusively of vole remains. Can be found on or near tussocks in fields, meadows and similar places (see page 207).

Eagle owl

Pellet is very large, approx. 4 cm in diameter and often 10 cm long, sometimes even longer. Primary contents are remains of small rodents, but often also remains of larger creatures such as hare or capercaillie. Found in mountain woodland and on rocks (see page 207).

Barn owl

Pellet is either *cylindrical* with blunt ends or almost *spherical*, and has a diameter of 2.5-3.5 cm. It is easily recognised, as it is covered with a dark grey crust that gives it a fairly smooth surface. The content is also typical in consisting of mouse and shrew remains. Found in churches, barns, ruins and similar places (see page 207).

Little owl

Pellet is fairly small, 2-5 cm long and approx. 1.5 cm thick; usually rounded at one end and pointed at the other. In spring and summer the owl feeds mostly on insects and earthworms, and this affects the pellet, which can be quite blue-black from beetle remains and may contain sand and earth particles from the guts of earthworms. The rest of the year the pellet is grey, containing remains of mice and small birds. Found in hollow trees and similar places (see page 207).

Birds of prey

In contrast to owls, the digestive juices of birds of prey can dissolve bones, so their pellets contain no bones, or only a few half-digested pieces. Another reason for the low bone content is also that birds of prey usually tear their prey apart and do not swallow large pieces of bone. This is also connected to the fact that birds of prey have a crop, an extension to the gullet, which acts as a reservoir, filling up when the stomach is full. When the crop is full, the gullet is blocked, and no pellets can be coughed up. Therefore it is important that the food should contain as few indigestible parts as possible. Pellets of birds of prey contain almost exclusively fur, small feathers, insect chitin, and – in contrast to owls – horn from beaks and claws. The food remains are usually fairly indeterminate, so unlike owl pellets, they provide little information on the birds' food choices. Pellets are found near nests, near resting places, and sometimes at feeding sites. Close identification is usually difficult.

Buzzard

Pellet is usually 6-7 cm long and 2.5-3 cm thick, cylindrical, with blunt ends or pointed at one end. It is grey and consists

mainly of firmly matted fur from small rodents. Found under tall trees and near fence posts in fields (see page 207).

Sparrowhawk

Pellet is 2-4 cm long and 1.2-1.7 cm thick. It consists of firmly matted small feathers. Primarily found along woodland edges (see page 207).

Goshawk

Pellet resembles that of sparrowhawk, but is larger, up to 6-7 cm long. Its content of fur and feathers usually comes from larger prey than that of the sparrowhawk.

A falcon's pellet.

Kestrel

Pellet is approx. 1.5 cm thick and 3-3.5 cm long. It is rounded at one end and pointed at the other; its content consists primarily of mouse fur, small feathers and remains of insects (see page 207).

Crow family

The pellets of members of the crow family are generally elliptical or egg-shaped, and contain a great deal of plant matter, mostly from various grass species, and often pieces of insect chitin. There are also nearly always small stones, swallowed by the birds to grind up seeds etc. in the gizzard. The pellet itself is usually yellowish and rather loose, falling apart easily. If the birds have eaten small mammals (usually as carrion), the pellet is firmer and darker, containing bones.

Crow

Pellet is 4-4.5 cm long and approx. 2 cm thick. Found near the nest, and in fields and on beaches (see page 206).

Rook

Pellet is 3-3.5 cm long and just under 2 cm thick. Usually found near the birds' colonies and in fields where they forage (see page 206).

Pellets at raven's roost.

Jackdaw

Pellet is approx. 3 cm long and 1-1.5 cm thick. Found primarily near nesting places (see page 206).

Magpie

Pellet is 3-3.5 cm long and 1.5-2 cm thick. Found primarily near nesting place, but may also be seen anywhere (see page 206).

Gulls

Gull pellets are spherical or short and cylindrical, sometimes rather pointed at one end. The content varies widely, consisting of either animal or vegetable food remains, or – as is often the case – a mixture of both.

The pellet is generally very loose if it consists of animal remains, e.g. fishbones, pieces of snail shells, shellfish and crabs. It falls apart very easily, and usually looks like a small crumbling heap. If it consists entirely, or largely, of plant remains, e.g. chaff, remains of berries etc, it will be firmer. This type of pellet frequently has a high content of insect remains, particularly from beetles.

In gull colonies near large cities, where gulls often forage on rubbish dumps, pellets often contain the strangest things, e.g. pieces of glass, rubber bands, plastic bags, silver paper and many other things, testimony both to the greed of gulls when they forage in flocks, and to the wastefulness of city life.

Gull pellets are mostly found in breeding colonies and at the birds' resting places

Herring gull's pellet, containing fish bones.

Common gull's pellet with cherry stones.

along the beach. Pellets of black-headed gull and common gull are also found in fields where the birds have foraged.

Black-headed gull
Pellet is 2.5-4 cm long and 1.5-2 cm thick. It may contain fishbones and remains of various beach creatures. This gull often forages on land, so its pellet often also contains chaff and other plant remains, e.g. bilberries and crowberries, making the pellet blue-black. It also often contains many insect remains, especially of beetles (see page 206).

Common gull
Pellet is 5-8 cm long and approx. 2 cm thick; its content is very similar to that of the black-headed gull. In areas where there are many cherries, its pellets may be composed almost entirely of cherry stones (see page 206).

Herring gull
Pellet is 2.5-3 cm thick and 3-5 cm long. It contains remains of fish, crabs, shellfish and snails, as well as plant remains (see page 206).

Storks and herons

Like birds of prey, storks' digestive juices can dissolve the bones of their prey, so they are rarely, if ever, found in their pellets. Fur, feathers, and chitin from insects, however, are well preserved.

Stork

The stork's pellet is more regular than that of the heron, and is usually 4-5.5 cm long and 2.5-3.5 cm thick. It often has a sweetish, cloying smell, and contains fur, feathers and insect remains. Storks also catch many earthworms, and the high content of sand found in the pellet comes largely from the worms' guts (see page 207).

Grey heron

The pellets vary widely in shape and size. They can be very regular round or oval balls of densely matted mammal fur, or more irregularly composed of more or less connected small balls of fur. Sometimes they consist of a loose mass of feathers. Usually most of the pellet is fur from small rodents, particularly field voles and water voles, but also shrews and moles. Insect chitin is also often found, while there is generally no trace of fish, for example, of which herons catch a great deal. The pellets are commonly found near the birds' resting places, and on beaches and similar places where they forage (see page 207).

OTHER
SIGNS

Tracks

Very few animals move around at random within their territory; on the contrary, they usually follow a network of paths or tracks that they know intimately, and can therefore use for a speedy escape if surprised. These tracks are often sharply defined in the terrain, and even the tracks of small, light creatures can be extremely firmly-trodden (see photograph on facing page). But as the tracks are mostly used at night, it must surely be the smell or scent left by the animals' earlier passage that guides them when they follow a track, rather than sight. The tracks will always follow the easiest route, determined by the prevailing conditions, so they often twist sharply, winding round tree stumps, stones and other obstacles. They may also follow paths and roads made by humans for certain distances.

Sometimes several species may use the same track or just a section of it. You may, for example, be fortunate enough to see signs of a hare and of a deer on the same track. A demonstration using a camera set up on a rodent track showed that several different species used the same track.

Large herbivores
Tracks of large herbivores can be clearly seen on the outer edges of woodland, from

Roe deer track over a salt marsh.

the shelter of which they venture out to forage in fields and meadows. The tracks will usually be most clearly defined near good foraging spots. Thus if you follow a hare's track away from cover, for example, it will be very clearly defined at first, but will eventually divide and become more and more indistinct.

Small rodents
Many small rodents create tracks that connect an underground tunnel system with feeding sites, or connect one hole with another. This is particularly marked in *field voles*, which live in dense grass. These tracks are often hidden at the base of plants, only visible if you push the grass aside. In winter

Rabbit track in the snow.

Winter tunnels of field vole.

they make corresponding tracks under the snow. These tracks are often lined with bitten-off pieces of grass, so when the snow melts in spring, they remain like fragile tunnels. *Water vole* tracks can be seen along streams and in bogs, and at rubbish dumps you can usually find distinct *brown rat* tracks, leading from their den close by the

dump right into the rubbish heap itself, where the animals forage. The *black rat* or roof rat, a considerably better climber than the brown rat, mostly keeps to the upper floors and roofs of buildings, where its comings and goings over the roof timbers are marked by a characteristic dark, greasy coating.

Beavers

A rather special type of track is the narrow channel which beavers dig from lakes through low-lying marshy areas, through which they transport gnawed-off twigs to their lodges and dams.

Gamebirds

In their movements through fences and hedges, these birds use tracks previously created by other animals, but when the ground is covered with snow, you can often find tracks made solely by pheasants and partridges.

A beaver channel.

Homes and hiding-places

Animals generally make their homes in a well-hidden or inaccessible spot, and they will usually be inconspicuous and therefore difficult to find. If, however, you are able to follow an animal's track, sooner or later you will come to its home or hiding-place. In the breeding season the adults' busy comings and goings with food for their young can give away the location of the home, and the autumn leaf-fall likewise discloses many animals' homes.

Few animals have a permanent home for use all through the year. A large majority have a home only in the breeding season, to protect their young, with perhaps a winter home for shelter from damp and cold, otherwise sleeping in constantly changing hiding-places. Some animals have no permanent abode even in the breeding season, but constantly change their sleeping place.

Birds' nests are by far the commonest homes we come across in nature. While in use, they are generally well hidden in undergrowth or the foliage of trees and bushes, but in the winter period many are easily visible. There is great variety in their appearance, and they are characteristic for each individual bird species in terms of position, size, construction and materials. It is unfortunately beyond the scope of this book to go into details of the nests of the many bird species.

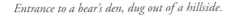

Entrance to a bear's den, dug out of a hillside.

A gamebird has left its sleeping-hollow.

Gamebirds often rest or sleep on the ground, making a bowl-shaped hiding-place in the vegetation, where there is generally a tell-tale heap of droppings. In cold climates, where the night temperature in winter is frequently so low that it is dangerous for gamebirds and others to spend the night up in the trees, they can often be seen digging down into the snow, seeking shelter from the cold.

Swallows' nest-building can also be seen in signs other than the nest itself: at the edges of partially-dried puddles in loamy areas it is sometimes possible to spot a number of small bird tracks and broad beakmarks. These are from *swallows*, fetching materials for their nests, which they make from straw

mixed with clay slurry. House martins also gather mud in similar fashion.

Like birds' nests, the homes of mammals vary greatly, and the following section can only describe some of the types of homes and hiding-places most frequently come across on walks in the countryside.

Homes on the ground

Deer and hares have no permanent homes, but sleep casually in suitable places in a simple resiing place or 'form' – as it is commonly termed – that is only used more than once in exceptional circumstances. Not even in the breeding season do these creatures have a permanent resting place, as the young are ready to leave their birthplace shortly after being born, and subsequently change home frequently.

Deer

Very few deer make anything special of their rest sites. They simply lie down to rest in a more or less hidden spot. Due to their weight, the vegetation at that place will remain firmly trampled, betraying the presence of the animal long after it has left. There will generally also be droppings, and from them and the size of the rest site it is often easy to determine the species of deer. The rest site is naturally considerably more clearly defined in snow, with a distinct print of the animal's body and limbs.

Roe deer rest sites differ somewhat from those of other deer, as this deer carefully scrapes leaves, twigs and often even vegetation away with its forehoofs, before lying down to rest on the bare ground.

Hares

A hare's form is a faint depression, often occurring naturally, with a strong resemblance to the imprint of a human knee, in soft earth, deeper and broader towards the back. The form is often scraped clean of leaves and suchlike, so the animal lies on the bare ground. However, forms where young are born are often lined with wool, plucked by the mother from her own fur. The form is normally by a clump of grass, a

A roe deer's lair scraped out of the snow. Compare this with the photograph on page 154.

the snow often having melted slightly due to the warmth of the animal. In the middle of the form an imprint of the long rear legs can often be seen. In deep snow the *mountain hare* will often dig a short, bow-shaped tunnel down into the snow right next to the form. As there is no form in the tunnel itself, this is thought to be a place of refuge, where the animal can shelter if attacked by a bird of prey or owl.

Homes above the ground

Some mammals make their homes in foliage, and at first sight these can be confused with birds' nests.

Squirrel

Hare's form in tall grass.

stone or something similar, that can provide shelter from the wind. The animal always lies with its rear end inwards, where the form is deepest and broadest, resting on the thick hair padding of the legs, with its rear legs pulled in under the body and its forelegs stretched forwards.

A hare lying in its form is very hard to spot, and, confident of this, the animal may often remain lying there under cover, until about to be stepped on. By carefully moving closer to the animal from the front, i.e. from the side to which the animal will jump, it is possible to get very close, sometimes so close that you can even touch it before it jumps.

In winter, the hare's form is generally just a scraped-out depression in the snow,

The squirrel, for instance, builds its home or drey in a tree, often close to the trunk, where one or more branches can support it. It is spherical, with a diameter of 20-50 cm. At the side is an entrance hole approximately 5 cm across, which the squirrel blocks up in bad weather, or when it has young and must leave the nest to look for food. Externally the drey consists of a loose weave of twigs, covered inside with a thick layer of grass, moss or fibres, which the squirrel has pulled off dead branches. Inside that is soft material, feathers, hair or whatever the squirrel has managed to get hold of.

The squirrel builds several nests; a solidly-constructed main drey, used for breeding and perhaps as a winter home, and two or three more primitive nests, used as occasional sleeping-places. Sometimes the squirrel

Red squirrel's drey.

builds nests in hollow trees, in birds' nesting-tekstboxes and similar places, where the nest will generally consist only of a lining.

A squirrel's drey somewhat resembles the spherical nest of the magpie, which consists of a solid base – constructed of twigs, clay and rootlets – covered by a vaulted roof of dry twigs. A magpie's nest is, however, considerably larger than that of a squirrel, and is generally located out among the branches rather than close to the trunk.

Harvest mouse

Harvest mice build two kinds of nest – summer nests and winter nests. The elaborately constructed summer nests are found up in the vegetation, generally 30-40 cm above the ground. The nest is spherical,

Grass split by harvest mouse for use in nest-building.

225

Harvest mouse's summer nest.

with a diameter of 8-10 cm and has a round entrance hole at the side. The nest material consists almost exclusively of blades of grass, which the mice split lengthways with their front teeth and carefully weave together. To support the nest, all nearby blades and stems are woven in, and as they are not bitten off, they retain their green colour throughout the summer, helping to camouflage the nest. When the vegetation withers in autumn, the nests stand out clearly like small balls of hay. The harvest mouse builds several summer nests, one of which is used for breeding. This is slightly larger than the others, and is lined. Summer nests are found in tall grass or other tall herbaceous plants, but they are also found at the bottom of dense bushes like hawthorn or blackthorn, and quite often on lower branches of coniferous trees.

The summer nests are often confused with birds' nests, e.g. the wren's spherical nest, but these will always contain some down.

Winter nests are located on the ground, in a tussock, or under a root or stone. Alternatively, the harvest mouse may dig short tunnels in the earth and establish its winter quarters there. The winter nest otherwise resembles the summer one, but is less elaborately and carefully built. In mild winters the mice sometimes use particularly well–padded summer nests, but these always seem to be in bushes or small trees.

Common dormouse

Amongst the members of the dormouse family, all of which hibernate, there are several species that build homes in trees and bushes in the summer. The common dormouse is a master of these, and its elegant home is equal to that of the elaborate, spherical nests of the wren and the long-tailed tit. The round or oval home, with a diameter of 10-15 cm and an entrance hole at the side, is positioned 1-4 m above the ground. The nest material can vary greatly, depending on local materials: hay, dry leaves, bark fibres, moss and lichen, carefully woven together. Inside, the home is lined with shredded plant matter and similar soft material. The

common dormouse's winter nest, in which it hibernates, is usually located in a hollow in the ground, under a root or stone, but may also frequently be found in hollow trees, and quite often in nest-boxes.

Garden dormouse

As its name suggests, this dormouse often appears in gardens, parks and orchards, where it builds a spherical home of twigs, leaves and moss, lined with grass, wool and other soft stuff. The summer home can be found in trees and bushes, but is often located in heaps of twigs, woodpiles, old bird or squirrel nests and hollow trees. Old nest-boxes are also sometimes used. The winter

Dormouse's nest built in a bramble thicket.

Field vole's nest.

home appears in the same places as that of the common dormouse. The garden dormouse often enters buildings, especially in autumn, where it stays in cellars and storerooms; in such places it need not hibernate.

Homes underground

Many mammals make their homes in the earth, usually a tunnel system with some degree of branching. In making these homes, they use three different methods to get rid of the loose earth excavated: 1) pushing it out to the sides, 2) throwing it upwards onto the surface to form mounds, 3) scraping it out of the entrance hole, where it is deposited in a flat, fan-shaped heap, and is often conspicuous.

As an individual species will usually only use one of these methods to remove excess earth, this is significant for identification. Other things to note are the size and position of the entrance hole, as well as any footprints or droppings in front. By investigating the roots that often protrude, it is often possible to find tufts of hair that reveal the inhabitant's identity.

To determine whether a home is in use

or has been abandoned, note whether the entrance hole displays fresh wear, and possibly new footprints, or whether it is overgrown, more or less filled with fallen leaves, or perhaps closed up with cobwebs. Sometimes one can simply smell whether a home is in use.

Rabbit

In contrast to the hare, the rabbit has an underground home, consisting of a nesting chamber, about 40-50 cm under the earth's surface. Around this stretches a complex system of tunnels with many holes. Earth is dug loose with the forepaws and then kicked backwards with the hind legs, ending up in a heap outside the hole. Some of the tunnels, however, are dug from inside, so no excavated earth is found in front of them. On the surface the holes are linked with tracks, often very clearly defined, and on these and around the holes one can always find the small round droppings characteristic of rabbits (see page 184). In contrast to hares, rabbits are social animals that normally live in colonies, in which the tunnel systems link up.

The dominant females in the warren create special breeding nests in blind tunnels within the colony itself, while the subordinate females' breeding nests are often in blind tunnels about 1 m deep on the colony fringes. The nest is lined with hay or hair, which the female pulls from her own coat. She stays in the breeding nest while the young are being suckled; when she does leave it, she closes up the entrance with earth, 'sealing' it with urine or droppings. This marking is respected by the other rabbits in the warren.

Rabbit holes on a sandy bank. Hollows with droppings can be seen at the side of the holes.

229

Molehills on a freshly-harrowed field.

Mole

Moles make three different types of tunnel in the earth. Two of them, breeding runs and surface runs, are fairly close to the surface. The third type, the permanent tunnels, where the nests are also to be found, lie deeper in the earth; it is these that are linked to molehills. The tunnels are slightly oval in cross section, about 5 cm wide and 4 cm high.

Breeding runs are open tunnels, like a little ditch, with thrown-up earth along both sides. They appear not only in the breeding season, but also when the mole is highly excited for some reason or another. When a mole digs down into the earth from the surface, it brings its forepaws in front of its snout, and as it pushes them downwards and outwards, it thrusts the earth to the side, pushing its snout into the hole thus created. If the mole continues in this way along the earth's surface instead of going deeper, this type of tunnel will form.

Surface runs are formed when the mole digs tunnels just below the soil surface, removing earth by pushing it into the air with its forepaws, so the ceiling of the tunnel is raised, making it stand out like a rampart on the surface.

The deeper permanent tunnels are roughly horizontal, with oblique tunnels leading from them to the surface, through which the loose excavated earth is thrust up to form molehills. The mole uses its left and right forepaws alternately to thrust the earth up. Movement can be observed when the earth is being pushed up; it appears in small jerks in the middle of the molehill, then tips over to the sides. In winter, when the molehills are slightly frozen, the pushed-up earth can be seen rising like a continuous column of the same diameter as the entry tunnel. In very loose earth, such as deep forest soils for example, the mole can make tunnels by pushing the earth out to the sides. In such places the home is not marked out on the surface in this way.

The mole's spherical nest, consisting of hay and leaves, is normally connected with the deep tunnels. However, in damp, low-lying areas it is often found in a giant mole-hill, which may be 0.5 m high and about 1.5 m in diameter.

When the mole leaves its tunnel system

Molehill. The earth that has been pushed up has partially retained the shape of the tunnel.

Mole's surface tunnel.

231

The mole and the water vole both make mounds, and these can be hard to tell apart. Here, however, the exit holes are visible. In the case of the mole this is in the mound itself (left), while the water vole forms its mound to one side of the hole (right).

to look for food on the surface, it always does so through one of the oblique tunnels through which it has pushed out earth, so the exit hole will always be at a molehill. These holes are rarely seen; this is because the mole closes up the hole after itself, apparently on its return.

Water vole

The water vole lives in an often deep and extensive tunnel system that greatly resembles that of the mole, in that the water vole also removes excavated earth by thrusting it up into a mound on the surface. However, the water vole's mounds vary greatly in size, and are more irregular in both shape and distribution than molehills. Also, in the summer period, when the water vole feeds on green surface vegetation, it is usually possible to find large holes leading down into the tunnel system with a diameter of 6-8 cm, and the vegetation is often gnawed away for a certain distance around the

opening. The holes are almost never connected to the mounds (see Mole), and there is not usually any scraped-out earth in front of the hole, as there is at rat-holes. In loose earth the water vole does not make mounds, but pushes the earth out to the sides.

The water vole's large, spherical nest is normally constructed in a special nesting chamber in the tunnel system, but in very damp areas it is often found above ground, in a clump of rushes, for example. It often uses grass or rushes as nest materials.

Sometimes, after the snow has melted in the spring, solid, branching 'sausages' of earth can be seen on the ground. These 'sausages', with a diameter of 6-8 cm and as much as several metres in length, are made by water voles. During the winter the water vole made tunnels in the lowest part of the snow; when extending its underground tunnels, it removed earth by pushing it into the snow tunnels. When the snow disappears

Holes and tunnels of water voles are usually found on riverbanks, which may be riddled with holes.

slowly through evaporation in clear, freezing weather, the 'sausages' remain as a beautiful cast of the tunnels.

'Earth sausages' occur when the water vole has filled its snow tunnels with earth.

Bank vole emerging from its hole by a tree root.

Rats

Brown rat: the nest is often found in buildings under floors, in cavity walls or between stacked items. Any available materials are used to build the nest, usually hay, straw, paper and bits of cloth. Outdoors the rat makes its home in an underground tunnel system, varying greatly in extent depending on conditions, but not generally going deeper than 40-50 cm. Usually there are several holes to each system, connected on the surface by clear, well-trodden tracks.

The rat is a decidedly social animal, often living in packs with common tunnel systems.

Rat-holes vary greatly in size, but are usually 6-8 cm in diameter and can be distinguished from the similarly-sized holes of the water vole by the fact that the excavated earth lies in a heap outside the hole. An exception to this is the so-called sewer-rat hole, which has no heap of earth. These holes originate from rats that have dug their way up from a sewer crack. The hole is made from below, and the excavated earth the rats have scraped into the sewer network through the crack has been carried away by the water. Often the amount of earth removed in this way by a rat is so large that there may be a marked subsidence of the surface.

Black rat (roof rat): the black rat does not dig tunnels and is not found out of doors in central and northern Europe.

Wood mouse

The wood mouse is commonly found on open land. It lives in a tunnel system, which is normally deep, often 1 m or more beneath the earth's surface. Connected to the tunnel system is a large nesting chamber, filled with finely shredded grass. The excavated earth is found in a large conical heap in front of the 3-4 cm holes. Sometimes there are also holes without earth, created when the mouse digs out from below. As the tunnels often reach down to the lighter earth layers below the humus, the excavated earth is often very conspicuous against the dark surface. The deep, branching tunnel systems are principally used in the winter. In the summer the mouse often digs simpler tunnel systems, closer to the surface, and sometimes the nest can be found above ground, in a dense tussock of grass, for example.

Other small mammals

Animals such as *shrews* and many other *small rodents* often make a home consisting of a spherical nest of hay, moss and similar plant matter, in naturally occurring cavities, for example in rotten tree stumps, under stones and fallen tree trunks, or on the ground in dense vegetation. They often establish their nests in short, fairly simple tunnel systems in the top layer of soil, which is loose enough to be pushed out easily to the sides. All that marks the tunnels on the surface is a little entrance hole. The homes of the different species are hard to distinguish from each other.

A lemming's entrance hole, with a clearly gnawed track leading to it.

Hamster

Hamsters dig tunnel systems underground. In contrast to the rabbit, the individual homes are not linked to each other, and each system is marked with a scent from special glands. The homes, however, are frequently near to each other. The burrows go down to a depth of about 2 m, and contain a nest lined with dry grass. There are also latrines and a storeroom. Storerooms have been found containing as much as 14 kg grain.

Alpine marmot

The alpine marmot is a social animal, and several individuals share a complex of burrows. These are usually established on sunny south- or west-facing mountain slopes. The alpine marmot normally prefers places where deposits of crumbled material lie

Hole of an alpine marmot.

A muskrat's lodge on a frozen lake. The entrance is under the ice.

stabilised at the foot of a rock wall, and where there is plenty of earth between large boulders. The tunnels can be as deep as 3 m, but about 1 m is most common. The main nesting chamber is an extension of the tunnel. It is lined with dry grass brought down in the summer and changed after the winter. Before hibernating, the marmot blocks the tunnel entrances with earth. This has the double advantage of making the entrances less visible and providing insulation.

Muskrat

The muskrat lives by lakes and ponds, and along rivers where the current is not too strong. It makes its home in the banks, where it digs branching tunnel systems with a tunnel diameter of 15-20 cm. It also often

builds a free-standing lodge of rushes and reeds in vegetation in shallow water. The lodge has a diameter of 1.5 m and can rise 1 m above the surface of the water. The entrance is underwater. As the plant matter used in the construction of the lodge is hollow, enough air gets into the lodge for the muskrat to be able to breathe, even in winter, when the water freezes.

Beaver

The beaver is a master builder among mammals, famed for its construction of dams and its elaborately-built lodges. While single or itinerant beavers dig tunnels into a bank and make a nest there, a pair of beavers will make their home in a so-called beaver lodge. This is built of pieces of branches ('beaver sticks' – see page 120), between which they pack earth, water plants and other plant matter. As the branches are tightly entangled, the lodge is extraordinarily solid and can be very large, as much as a couple of metres high and about 15 m round. If it is built out on the water, in a pond, for example, it is often round, but lodges on a bank have an elongated shape. This is because the entrance must be underwater, so the lodge must therefore have an extension going out into

A beaver's lodge built by a winding stream.

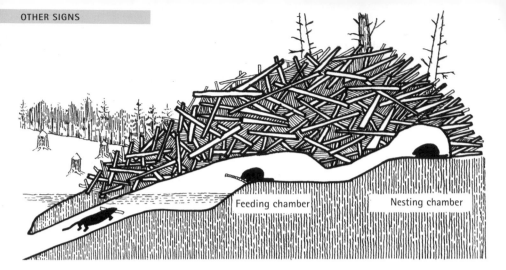

Diagram of a beaver lodge in cross section. △

Feeding chamber

Nesting chamber

▽*Beaver dam.*

the water. Inside the lodge is a roomy nesting chamber lined with hay and wood chips.

Beavers living near running water often build dams to stem the current of the water and flood the surrounding flat areas, giving the beavers easier access to the nearby trees (see also page 120). The dams, which can be over 100 m long, are constructed of branches, earth and water plants, and are extremely firm and solid. Two or three dams are often built one after another, with fairly short distances between them.

Fox

The construction of a fox's burrow or den ('earth') varies greatly. It can be a simple burrow with a single hole under a stone or a tree root. Simple holes in canal banks, railway embankments or in open fields with no cover are also common. Even artificial sites, such as concrete pipes may be used. On the other hand, it may also be a fairly complicated tunnel complex with several exits, of which only a few are used regularly. During the digging, the fox transports the excavated earth to the exit, where it is spread out, forming a fan-shaped heap. In newly-established dens, the entrance hole is rather narrow, 25 cm in diameter, while old dens that have been used for decades, perhaps centuries, have much larger holes.

As foxes produce a sharp, acrid smell, it is often possible to determine whether or not a burrow is inhabited by putting your head into the entrance hole and sniffing. If there are young in the burrow, there will generally be some remains of meals, bones, feathers and suchlike, lying in front of the hole, and as foxes like to play and sun

A fox's den, with the excavated earth characteristically spread out in a fan shape in front of the hole.

themselves out in the open in good weather, the vegetation round about the hole will be trampled down. The urine and droppings of foxes, as well as the remains of their meals, act as plant fertiliser, and, particularly in spring, the growth of vegetation in front of fox and badger burrows is considerably lusher than elsewhere in the vicinity. There will often also be some species typical of rich soils – such as nettles.

For homes common to foxes and other animals see below under badger.

Badger

The sett of a badger resembles the fox's earth to some extent, but can be even larger, so the excavated earth on slopes may form terraces. Badgers shift the excavated soil farther away from the hole than do foxes, creating ditches of varying depth in the earth heap in front of the hole. In addition, unlike the fox, the badger uses hay, withered

239

leaves and moss as nesting material, and outside the sett there will often be bits dropped by the badger while dragging them in. The badger also lacks the strong scent of the fox, and you can generally find small characteristic holes around the home, scraped by the badger to use as a latrine (see also page 188). Both species may use the same burrow complex alternately, and in rare cases they may even share the same burrow. *Martens, otters* and *cats* may also make their homes in these complexes. Their signs can be found in the scrapings.

Polecat and mink

Polecats and mink use existing holes, but sometimes extend them, causing scrapings to appear.

A badger's sett, with the characteristic furrow.

Signs of particular behaviour

Fraying

A particular kind of trace, which is very conspicuous and easily recognised, is that of *fraying by deer*. This refers to the marks made by deer in various circumstances with their antlers – on trees and bushes, and occasionally on stiff plants.

Except for reindeer, whose females also have antlers, these grow only on the males, who use them primarily for fighting with each other. The antlers probably also act as a visible, external sign of strength, to warn off opponents and attract females.

Antlers are a pair of bony growths, branching to varying degrees. They are shed each year, after which a new – gener-

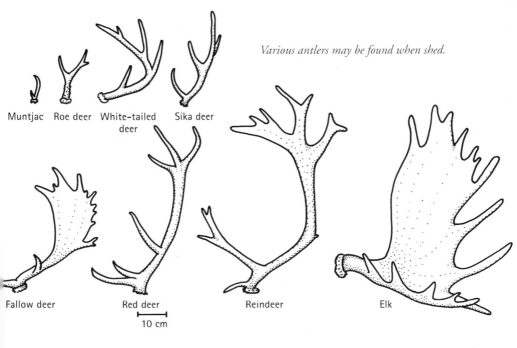

Various antlers may be found when shed.

Muntjac   Roe deer   White-tailed deer   Sika deer

Fallow deer   Red deer   Reindeer   Elk

10 cm

ally larger – set of antlers grows. The shed antlers are nearly always found singly and are generally easy to identify, as each deer species has its own characteristic antler shape.

While growing, the antlers are covered with a heavily blood-filled, hairy skin, called velvet. When the antlers are fully formed and completely ossified, the blood vessels shrink. A fluid layer forms beneath the velvet, making it loose and allowing it to come off easily when the deer rubs and chafes (frays) its antlers against thin, resilient tree trunks, bushes or stiff plants. This tears the bark off, making it hang in long tatters, and the lateral branches are snapped or torn off completely. Since the

Discarded roe deer antler.

Fraying by red deer (left), roe deer (middle) and reindeer (right).

velvet is already loose, fraying itself is quite a rapid process – the antlers are generally clean within a few hours. The deer eat the velvet, so it is rare to find any remains of it at the fraying spot. The antlers are completely white once the velvet has been removed, but quickly acquire a brownish colour, which is apparently mainly due to the sap of the tree or bush the deer used for fraying.

Red, fallow and *sika deer* and *elk* fray their velvet in late summer to early autumn, while *roe deer* do this in spring.

Particularly in the rutting season, deer perform another kind of marking by excitedly butting and striking their antlers on bushes and even large trees, so the bark gets broken up in deep furrows or flakes off. It has been observed that this behaviour occurs in deer that have just met a rival; it may thus be regarded as a working-off of excessive aggression. These activities, which are often very violent and can be almost like a fight with the object in question, often involve attacking the object from all sides. Other kinds of fraying, by contrast, are always one-sided.

Roebuck differ from other deer in that they continue fraying throughout the summer, even though the velvet is soon removed from the antlers. This behaviour is part of the deer's marking of territory and is therefore often called territorial fraying.

Sharpening

To maintain their claws, *cats* sharpen them on any fairly hard, tough material. Tree trunks are often used, with elder apparently being a favourite. As they use the same spot over a long period, the bark can eventually come right off. It is important for cats that their claws always be pointed and sharp, and the outer horny layer of each claw is regularly shed. They scratch at the bark in order to remove this layer. By looking closely it is sometimes possible to find these torn-off horny layers.

Bears also sharpen their claws.

Elder trunk marked by a cat sharpening its claws.

Scent marking and wallowing

Because mammals have an acute sense of smell, they often use *scent marking*. Many species have special glands that produce a secretion with a scent particular not only to the species but also to the individual animal. The glands may be concentrated in special scent organs found on the animals' feet, from which the secretion is deposited in the tracks – as in roe deer, for example. They can also be on the head or body, often near the tail, from where the secretion is deposited at especially strategic points, the animal actively rubbing the secretion onto the vegetation or the ground. Scent organs of this kind include the gland sac at the base of the badger's tail, the anal sac of the marten, the frontal (forehead) scent gland of the roe deer and the pre-orbital glands below the eyes of red deer.

Some scent organs function all year round, while others only develop in the sexually mature animal, and are chiefly functional in the rutting season.

Scent marking can also be done using urine and droppings. Many animals add special scent secretions to their excreted waste when depositing it.

Because of our relatively poor sense of

Scent organs of deer and fox.

The fox marks its territory etc. by placing its droppings in a prominent position.

Ring caused by roe deer.

smell we very rarely notice the scent markings of animals; we are only aware of them if they are particularly pronounced, like the urine markings of the fox. However, it is possible to infer from the positioning of certain animals' products, e.g. fox (pages 187 and 203) and rabbit (page 184), that they have been used for scent marking, as described in the sections on urine and droppings. In some cases the animals will also leave visible signs with the scent marking. This applies particularly, for example, to the roebuck, which carefully marks out its territory by conspicuous fraying, then rubs the frayed spots with secretions from the gland at the base of its antlers. The majority of roe deer frayings we come across are territorial rather than for removal of velvet (see page 241).

In the roe deer's mating season it is sometimes possible to see distinctive, well-trampled, circular tracks. They are formed as one of the final parts of the mating display, in which the doe moves round in a circle, closely followed by the buck. Such rings, often round a bush, a tree stump, a stone or similar, are generally circular or elliptical, and relatively small, but vary in both shape and size, depending on conditions. In some cases the deer use the same ring year after year. Fawns at play also make rings, and these are difficult to distinguish from the adults' rings if no hoofprints are visible.

In the breeding period it is possible to find hollows at the rutting grounds of red and fallow deer and elks. These are formed by the males, using their forelegs and antlers to throw earth aside to create a depression, into which the deer spray semen and urine.

Mixed with rainwater, this eventually forms a smelly mud bath, in which they roll and trample around, or 'wallow'. The smell from such hollows, so powerful as to be clearly noticeable even at a distance, is important in that it attracts and excites the females, who sometimes also wallow there. In deer-parks with a dense population of red or fallow deer, the fallow bucks in particular establish such hollows quite near to each other, and here it is often possible to observe fighting between the stags.

As well as these mating hollows, red deer have another type of *wallowing place*, where they take mud baths. These occur in bogs, by the shores of lakes and similar places, and are used a great deal by both sexes throughout most of the year. The significance of these is unclear, but they are most probably linked to skin care. The mud may also protect against biting insects. As the wallowing places are often in spots where the deer could just as well have bathed in clean water, it is unlikely that the mud baths are taken for cooling purposes.

Elk may have similar wallowing places, but they are unknown for *roe deer* and *fallow deer*.

Wild boar, like domestic pigs, greatly enjoy wallowing, and in areas where they are common you frequently come across their wallowing places. There will often be a tree nearby that shows clear signs of thorough rubbing by the animal after bathing. This sort of sign may also sometimes be seen at deer wallowing sites.

Red deer wallowing site.

Fighting and displaying

The numerous tufts of fur from *hares* found in certain fields in spring have nothing to do with moulting, but result from the extremely violent mating fights, in which they tear large tufts of fur from each other. Such fights often involve unreceptive females chasing off males.

On saltmarshes, often on a slightly raised plateau with dry ground, it is sometimes possible to see a number of circular spots with a diameter of up to 50-60 cm, where the vegetation has been trampled or completely worn away and dotted with a thin layer of white, smeared droppings (see next page). This is the lekking ground of *ruffs* and *reeves*, a mating arena. When the mating season approaches, the males gather here, where they each have precisely set boundaries, to hop and dance, carrying out feints on their neighbours. Occasionally a female appears in the arena; she selects a male and mates with him, before disappearing again.

The *great snipe*, which breeds in north-

Ruffs on their lekking ground, with patches of grass worn away.

Dust baths

east Europe, has a similar social mating game. It lives by bogs and marshes, and its arena is on rugged or tussocky terrain. Other species with similar behaviour include the *black grouse*, whose leks take place on open ground on heathland, in bogs or meadows, and the *capercaillie*, whose arenas are found in forest clearings. In many places the mating games of these birds, particularly of the black grouse, begin at a time when there is still snow on the ground, so you can often see how the males have danced with dragging wings, and where they have fought each other.

Near built-up areas one often sees *sparrows* taking dust baths in fine, dry earth. After perhaps loosening the earth with its beak, the bird lies down and flaps its wings to get the dust in between its feathers. Eventually this creates a hemispherical depression. This phenomenon, which forms part of the birds' feather-care, is also observed in other birds, e.g. larks. It is also fairly common in *gamebirds*, and can frequently be seen in poultry, where it may be seen that these birds use their legs as well as their beaks to make their dust baths. Dust hollows of gamebirds are usually found in sunny, south-facing spots, with dry, fine earth.

A pheasant's dusting site – the bowl-shaped depression in the ground in the centre of the picture.

Duck moulting site by a lake.

Moulting of fur and feathers

Very often you find signs connected to the moulting of fur or feathers. Generally these will be tufts of fur or single feathers, lying here and there, but sometimes you may also come across larger quantities. Many *ducks* have special moulting places along the shoreline, which they seek out in the moulting season; often each species has its own particular area. At such places you can often find large quantities of feathers washed ashore. Large collections of feathers can also be observed in areas with colonies of breeding birds, and on saltmarshes and similar places used by seagulls as roosting sites.

Feathers

Feathers are found in many places, bearing witness not only to the presence of a particular species of bird, but often also to various activities. Identifying which species the feathers come from is often difficult, and may require a thorough knowledge of birds. A good handbook on birds is very useful.

It is generally the large feathers, i.e. flight feathers, tail feathers and coverts on the wings and body that allow the easiest identification. The plates on the following pages show various examples of typical feathers from common species of birds.

One group of birds of which you can find many feathers is ducks. The various duck species have particular sites for moulting along the coasts and at lakes, and particularly in late summer and autumn large quantities of duck feathers are washed ashore (see photograph on page 249). The drake's lustrous body feathers are characteristic, and with perhaps a secondary feather with its boldly-coloured speculum, it is often possible to make a firm identification.

A dense collection of feathers may also

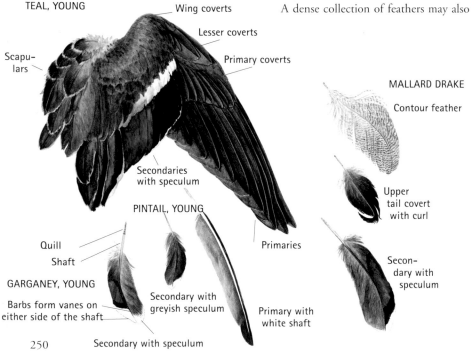

TEAL, YOUNG

Wing coverts

Lesser coverts

Scapulars

Primary coverts

MALLARD DRAKE

Contour feather

Secondaries with speculum

PINTAIL, YOUNG

Upper tail covert with curl

Quill

Shaft

Primaries

Secondary with speculum

GARGANEY, YOUNG

Barbs form vanes on either side of the shaft

Secondary with greyish speculum

Primary with white shaft

Secondary with speculum

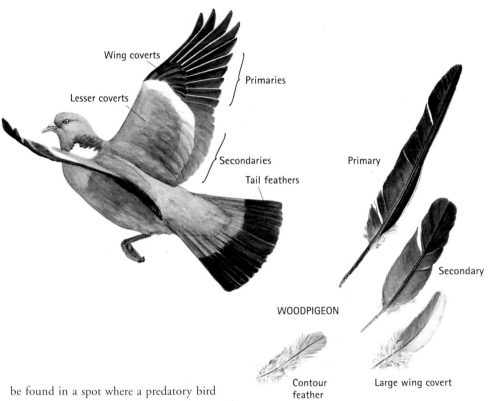

Wing coverts

Lesser coverts

Primaries

Secondaries

Tail feathers

WOODPIGEON

Primary

Secondary

Contour
feather

Large wing covert

be found in a spot where a predatory bird or mammal has eaten a bird. Thus the white and grey feathers of a wood pigeon may be found on the ground or on a tree stump, where it has been eaten by perhaps a goshawk. After striking the pigeon in the air, the hawk carries it to a safe site, and plucks out the feathers by the roots, leaving beak marks on the feather shafts (see page 159).

It is less common to find the remains of birds that have been the prey of animals such as foxes, since they normally drag their prey away to their hiding-places. Any feather remains you do find, at least the larger feathers, will have been bitten off,

TAWNY OWL

Primary

Secondary

251

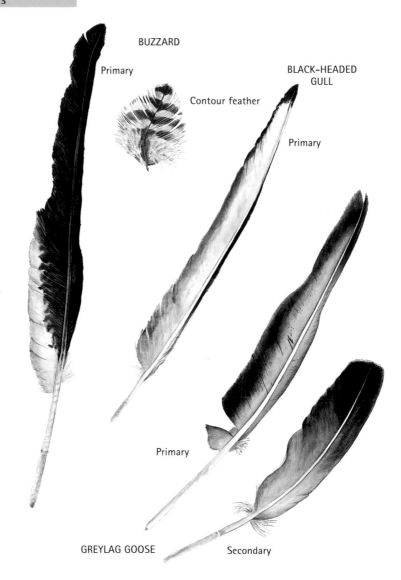

BUZZARD

Primary

Contour feather

BLACK-HEADED
GULL

Primary

Primary

GREYLAG GOOSE

Secondary

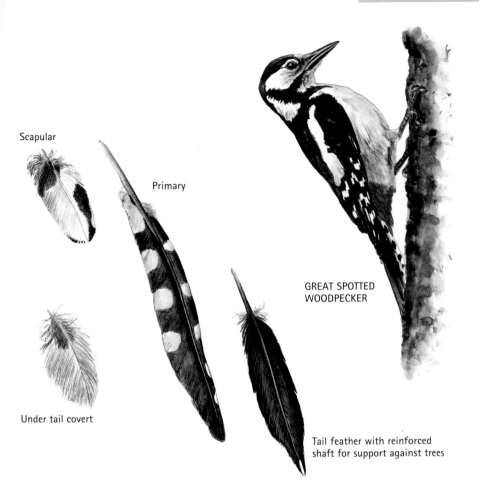

Scapular

Primary

GREAT SPOTTED
WOODPECKER

Under tail covert

Tail feather with reinforced
shaft for support against trees

the tip of the shaft remaining in the bird (see page 159).

Smaller bird species – including the many species of passerine – are important prey for various species of predatory birds and animals.

Plucked feathers may also be found as the remains of a sparrowhawk kill. Despite the colourful plumage of many passerines, such feathers may be very hard to identify. The feathers generally give only a downy and greyish impression. The intense colour of many small birds comes primarily from the density of their plumage; a single feather merely appears dull and less colourful. The following page shows examples of some of the most colourful or contrasting feathers of small birds.

253

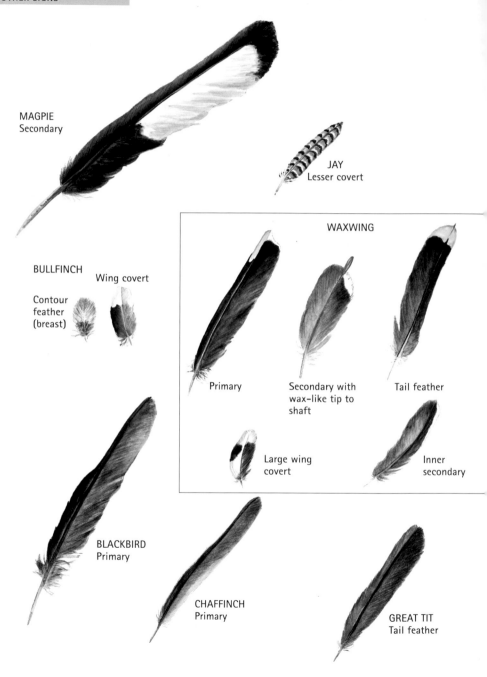

MAGPIE
Secondary

JAY
Lesser covert

WAXWING

BULLFINCH

Wing covert

Contour
feather
(breast)

Primary

Secondary with
wax-like tip to
shaft

Tail feather

Large wing
covert

Inner
secondary

BLACKBIRD
Primary

CHAFFINCH
Primary

GREAT TIT
Tail feather

ACKNOWLEDGEMENTS
AND INDEX

Photographic credits

Eric Dragesco, Switzerland: 48 right, 56 left, 96 right, 187 right, 190 top left, 198 top, 211 left

Bert Wiklund, Denmark: 26, 27, 68 left, 77 right, 93, 102, 148 left, 150, 161, 170 top, 242 bottom centre

Biofoto, Denmark
Carsten Bang: 197 bottom
Peter Marling: 33
Knud Garmann: 40, 84 right, 182
Niels Peter Holst Hansen: 49, 59 top, 67 right, 170 bottom left, 244
Lars Geil: 38 top, 60, 68 right, 76, 78 bottom, 83 left, 91, 95 left, 96 top left, 139, 168, 170 bottom right, 192 bottom, 194 bottom right, 196th, 213
Sune Holt: 38 bottom
Elvig Hansen: 55, 67 centre, 81, 82, 83 right, 84 left, 130, 133, 138 bottom right, 151, 164, 172 bottom right, 175, 180, 187 top left, 187 bottom left, 193 top, 194 top right, 202, 209, 226, 249 bottom
Kaj Haldberg: 53 bottom, 169 top
Lars Serritslev: 65 bottom, 126 right
Anders Tvevad: 65 top, 224
J. Plamrech: 67 left
Jens Kirkeby: 73
J.O. Ravn-Nielsen: 87 left
Hans Bjarne Hansen: 87 right, 88 top
Gerth Hansen: 90, 195, 197 top, 220 top

Arthur Christiansen: 92, 128, 152, 171
Ole Gabrielsen: 96 bottom
Benny Génsbøl: 136, 149
Hanne and Jens Eriksen: 173
Kaj Boldt: 240
Ib Trap-Lind: 233 top
S. Halling: 185 bottom
Erik Thomsen: 189, 190 bottom, 200, 208, 212, 214, 227, 234, 242 top, 248
Karsten Schnack: 143 left
Niels Westergaard Knudsen: 138 bottom left, 145, 218

Biofoto, Norway
Einar Hugnes: 46, 88 bottom, 89 right, 220 bottom
Lars Andreas Dybvik: 66, 123 top left and right
Kim Abel: 134, 242 bottom right
Torbjörn Moen: 154, 165 top
Stig Sund: 163 right
Torgeir Krokan: 166
Øystein Søby: 196 left
Bengt Silfverling: 221

Luonnonkuva Arkisto, Finland
Tuovnikoski Tuoma: 51
Heikki Willsmo: 54 top
Jouko Kuosmanen: 61 left
Harri Pulli: 163 left
Heikki Nikki: 198 bottom
Peritti Alaja: 233 bottom

Naturfotograferne, Norway
Tor Lundberg: 8, 71, 162
Lennart Mathiasson: 43 right, 167 top
Alf Linderheim: 44, 57, 61 bottom right, 127, 188 bottom, 238

Tommie Jacobsson: 54 bottom
Sixten Jonsson: 56 right, 61 top right, 184 left, 199 top
Ola Jennersten: 59 bottom
Viking Olsson: 63
Ulf Risberg: 70 left, 89 left, 94, 169 bottom, 188 top, 191
Bo Kristiansson: 70 right
Arne Schmitz: 72
Lars Jarnemo: 77 left, 123 bottom, 140, 219, 242 bottom left
Jan Töve: 79
Bengt Ekman: 80
Hilding Mickelsson: 86
Janos Jurka: 95 right, 120 bottom
Jan Grahn: 107 right
Folke Hårrskog: 126 left
Tore Hagman: 135
Göran Hansson: 143 right
Torbjörn Lilja: 147
Bo Brannhage: 148 right
Ove Andersson: 185 top, 235 left
Klas Rune: 190 bottom, 211 right, 229
Per-Olov Eriksson: 193 bottom left
Jan Johannesson: 230
Björn Uhr: 237
Hans Ring: 247

Samfoto, Norway
Pål Hermansen: 64, 107 left
Dagrinn Skjelle: 69
Rolf Sørensen: 78 top
Stig Tronvold: 165 bottom
Jon Østeng Hov: 199 bottom
Dag Røttereng: 222
J.B. Olsen & R. Sørensen: 245

All other photographs are by Preben Bang

Index